The flavour of Hong Kong

Revised Edition

香港風味

4C

Four Corners Publishing Company, Hong Kong

All colour photography and the illustrations on pages 15, 20, 56 and 78
by Benno Gross Associates, Hong Kong. Copyright held by Four
Corners Publishing Co. (Far East) Ltd.
The reproduction of photographs on pages 30, 95 and 98 by courtesy of
the Hong Kong Tourist Association.
The print 'Fruit and Vegetable Trading in D'Aguilar Street, 1870', which
appears on the endpapers of the book, is reproduced by courtesy of the
Hong Kong Museum of History.

Design: Pat Printer Associates, Hong Kong.

Typesetting: United Artists Typesetting, Hong Kong

Colour separation: Daiichi Seihan, Hong Kong

Printing: Paramount Press, Hong Kong

Published by Four Corners Publishing Co. (Far East) Ltd.
        Suite 15A, 257 Gloucester Road, Hong Kong

ISBN 85623010 3 Copyright© 1977, Four Corners

Edited by Kenneth Mitchell

Revised Edition

The flavour of Hong Kong

Revised Edition

香港風味

Edited by

Kenneth Mitchell

Contents

Introduction

To attempt to capture the 'flavour' of a large, modern metropolis in a modest cookbook, may seem an over-ambitious venture, yet, that is indeed what I have tried to do. Not that I believe for one moment that the selection of recipes which follow come close to comprising an exhaustive list of what Hong Kong has to offer, but I do believe that the choice represents a sufficient cross section to justify the title.

Certain omissions have been deliberate; for instance, this edition concerns itself only with Hong Kong's Chinese flavours, and disregards completely, all the other Asian and International cuisines, which are to be found in abundance, and which are of such a high standard, as to make this city a delight to gourmets of all inclinations. And, even within the area of Chinese food alone, there are, of necessity, all too many obvious gaps, for it would require a volume many times the size of this, to even come close to giving compre-

hensive coverage to the multitude of culinary delights available.

For Hong Kong abounds with places to eat, from simple street stalls to beautifully appointed restaurants atop luxury hotels, and it is from a cross section of these that the majority of the recipes within were obtained. Many were supplied by the chefs themselves, and are offered exactly as given, although in certain cases, deliberate changes have been made in order to achieve some form of standardization, and to direct the book toward the domestic kitchen.

Also the variety of Chinese cuisines to be experienced in Hong Kong seems endless, for while it is true that an extremely large percentage of the population have their origins in the neighbouring province of Kwangtung, resulting in a great predominance of the classical, and best known, Cantonese style of cooking, nevertheless the hot and spicy flavours of Szechuan and Shanghai, the delicate tastes of Swatow, the simple Hakka foods, and the highly favoured Peking cuisine, are all readily available. All offering their own distinctive flavours, and all playing their part in making this fantastic and unique city, the world's culinary centre for Chinese food.

For those not accustomed to Chinese cooking, it may, at first, appear to be extremely difficult and time-consuming, but it should be appreciated that most of the work lies in the initial preparations, while the actual cooking is usually simple, and generally involves little time. Of course there are exceptions, and one or two of the recipes inside may appear complicated at first glance, however I feel sure that with a little patience (and, perhaps, at the beginning, a certain amount of good humour!) all will prove practial. Home cooked Chinese meals most often consist of several dishes served simultaneously, and usually allow for one main course per person, with a soup, and a rice or noodle dish, being served in addition. However one of the delights of serving Chinese food, is the flexibility offered, so that personal tastes and preferences become all important, and the number and order of dishes, may be altered at will, with quantities adjusted accordingly. For this reason it was not considered practical to indicate a number of servings for each recipe. I feel sure that with just a little experimenting, and perhaps a small amount of improvisation (an essential ingredient in any good kitchen) excellent results will be achieved.

I wish you many happy hours of both cooking and enjoying the results.

K.M.

Utensils

The one utensil common to every Chinese kitchen is the 'wok', and although its use is not absolutely essential to bring about excellent results, it will without doubt make Chinese cooking decidedly easier, and also more fun. It is, I believe, the one addition that should be made to every kitchen, that presently is only equipped for the preparation of Western style cuisine. Every other necessity should already be there, and a few refinements can be bought later if required. The main attraction of the wok is its versatility, for it can be used for deep frying, stewing and steaming in addition to its most common use in Chinese cooking, that of stir-frying. Also the wok, with its small base area, where the heat is concentrated, and its deep sloping sides, allows for the simultaneous cooking of many ingredients without the use of numerous pans and the continual removing and keeping warm of ingredients which may require less cooking time than others.

Ingredients

Certain changes have been made in a few of the original recipes, and, as a result, it is unlikely that any ingredient will prove too difficult to obtain, even outside Asia. While certainly, some items may not be found in the village or suburban shop, they should be easy to find in the nearest large city, in supermarkets or Chinese supply stores. One ingredient which is used frequently in the following recipes is Chinese wine, and rather than buy this for only occasional use, it is suggested that dry sherry be substituted. Where important changes have been made, the explanations appear beneath the respective recipes.

Weights & Measures

Most weights and measures throughout this book are in metric, but any ingredient under 25 grams (25 g) or 25 millilitres (25 ml) has been indicated in spoons. Also where it was considered practical certain quantities were given by number; for example 6 dried Chinese mushrooms, and 2 spring onions BUT 1 tablespoon chopped spring onion.

For those who think and work in Imperial measures, there is a quick and simple conversion to keep in mind. That is taking 25 grams as being equal to 1 ounce, and 25 millilitres as being equal to 1 fluid ounce. However this is not an accurate conversion, and while quite satisfactory with small quantities, tends to become impractical as weights and measures become greater. The table gives the nearest gram/millilitre equivalent for 1 to 20 ounces/fluid ounces, and indicates the difference between the Imperial and U.S. pint.

Ounces/fluid ounces	Approx. g. and ml. to nearest whole figure	Ounces/fluid ounces	Approx. g. and ml. to nearest whole figure
1	28	11	311
2	57	12	340
3	85	13	368
4	113	14	396
5	142	15	428
6	170	16 (American pint)	456
7	198	17	484
8	226	18	512
9	255	19	541
10	283	20 (Imperial pint)	569

The art of using chopsticks, which at first may appear difficult, is, in reality, easily mastered with a small amount of practice. The added enjoyment of eating Chinese food this way, makes the slight effort of learning well worth while.
Grip one of the chopsticks in a fixed and firm position, then take the second one, and manipulate it as you would a pencil. In no time at all you will be picking up the smallest morsels with ease.

Dim Sum
點心

During the morning and at lunchtime,
a very popular feature of many of
Hong Kong's Cantonese restaurants is
the serving of Dim Sum, a seemingly
endless variety of small dishes, served
in the traditional manner by girls
carrying trays or pushing carts, and
calling out the names of the various
dishes as they weave their way through
crowded tables. Because Dim Sum
depends so much on a wide selection
of dishes it is not always practical to
serve at home. However one or two of
the items can be served as snacks or
small starters. Dim Sum is Cantonese
in origin, and strictly speaking
Shrimp Toast and Onion Cakes, both
from Northern cuisines, do not belong
in this section, but again both are
excellent ways of starting a meal, and
so have been included here.

8

Onion Cakes

4 spring onions
200 g plain flour
50 g melted lard
1 tablespoon sesame oil
½ teaspoon salt
½ teaspoon white pepper
100 ml peanut oil

Chop the spring onions into small pieces. Sift the flour into a large bowl, and add just sufficient boiling water to produce a thick sticky dough. Add the melted lard and half the sesame oil, and knead until the dough is smooth. Roll out on a lightly floured surface, and spread the chopped spring onions on top. Season with the salt and pepper, and sprinkle over the remaining sesame oil. Roll up, and cut into 2 inch pieces, then flatten each piece, sealing the edges to retain the onion inside. Heat the oil in a wok, or frying pan, and fry the onion cakes until golden brown.

Shrimp Toast with Sesame Seeds

250 g fresh shrimps
½ inch knob fresh ginger
1 clove garlic
1 egg white
2 teaspoons cornstarch
½ teaspoon salt
freshly ground black pepper
1 tablespoon Chinese wine

6 slices white bread
30 g sesame seeds
500 ml vegetable oil

Shell and de-vein the shrimps, and chop very finely. Crush the ginger and garlic. Beat the egg in a mixing bowl, and add the shrimps, ginger, garlic, cornstarch, salt, pepper and Chinese wine. Mix together thoroughly to form a smooth paste. Spread the prawn paste evenly on the slices of bread, and sprinkle over the sesame seeds. Heat the oil in a wok, or large frying pan, until almost smoking, then deep fry until the bread turns a dark golden brown. Remove from the oil, drain thoroughly, and cut into quarters.

Steamed Buns with Pork Filling

200 g roasted pork
2 spring onions
25 ml vegetable oil
2 teaspoons sugar
50 ml oyster sauce
1 tablespoon light soya sauce
¼ teaspoon white pepper
2 teaspoons cornstarch

Dough:
100 g sugar
25 g fresh yeast
400 g plain flour

Cut the pork into small dice, and finely chop the spring onions. Heat the oil in a wok, or frying pan, add the onions, and stir over medium heat for 1 minute. Add the pork, sugar, oyster sauce, soya sauce and pepper, and simmer gently for a further 2 minutes. Mix the cornstarch with a small quantity of cold water, and stir into the mixture. Remove from the pan, and allow to cool.

To make the dough, melt the sugar in 100 ml. of warm water, sprinkle in the yeast, mix well and allow to ferment for 5 minutes. Sift the flour into a large bowl, make a well in the centre, and slowly add the fermented yeast. Stir in to mix thoroughly, and knead firmly for 10 minutes, then cover with a cloth, and let stand for 45 minutes. Turn out the dough onto a lightly floured surface, and shape into a roll, 2 inches in diameter. Cut the roll into 1 inch pieces, flatten out with the hands, and set aside.

To cook, spoon a small quantity of the pork mixture onto a piece of dough, and fold up the edges to form a bun, leaving a small opening at the top. Place in a tightly sealed container, and steam for 8-10 minutes.

Steamed Prawn 'Wan Tun' Dumplings

12 frozen wun tun wrappers
250 g fresh prawns
2 dried Chinese mushrooms
2 water chestnuts
2 spring onions
1 teaspoon light soya sauce
1 teaspoon dark soya sauce
¼ teaspoon white pepper
dash monosodium glutamate
1 egg, beaten
2 teaspoons peanut oil

Shell and de-vein the prawns, and place through a very fine meat grinder. Soak the mushrooms in warm water for 30 minutes, remove and discard the hard stems, and cut into shreds. Finely chop the water chestnuts and spring onions, mix with the prawns and mushrooms, and season with the soya sauce, white pepper and monosodium glutamate. Spread the wrappers on a lightly greased surface, and spoon on portions of the mixture. Fold into small dumplings, and seal with the beaten egg. Place on a sheet of greaseproof paper, sprinkle over the peanut oil, and steam in a tightly sealed container for 10 minutes.

Fried Meat Dumplings

12 frozen wun tun wrappers
75 g fresh shrimps
300 g minced pork
50 g minced fish
25 g lard
2 teaspoons sugar
½ teaspoon salt
dash monosodium glutamate
freshly ground black pepper
1 teaspoon sesame oil
1 tablespoon cornstarch
1 egg, beaten
500 ml vegetable oil

Place the wun tun wrappers in a warming oven to thaw out. Shell and de-vein the shrimps, chop very finely, and mix with the minced pork and fish. Heat the lard in a wok, or shallow frying pan, and sauté the mixture for 2-3 minutes. Add the sugar, salt, monosodium glutamate, pepper and sesame oil, and continue to stir over medium heat for a further 2 minutes. Add cornstarch mixed with a little cold water, blend in well, then remove from heat and allow to cool. Spread the wrappers on a flat greased surface, and spoon equal portions of the mixture onto each. Fold into a triangle shape, seal the edges with the beaten egg, and deep fry in very hot vegetable oil until golden brown.

Spring Rolls

12 spring roll wrappers
6 dried Chinese mushrooms
150 g bamboo shoots
150 g fresh prawns
100 g roasted pork
25 ml peanut oil
1 tablespoon Chinese wine
1 tablespoon light soya sauce
½ tablespoon dark soya sauce
2 teaspoons sugar
½ teaspoon salt
¼ teaspoon white pepper
dash monosodium glutamate
½ tablespoon cornstarch
1 egg, beaten
500 ml vegetable oil

Place the spring roll wrappers in a warming oven to thaw out. Soak the mushrooms in warm water for 30 minutes; remove, drain and discard the hard stems. Boil bamboo shoots in water for 20 minutes, then remove and drain thoroughly. Cut the mushrooms, bamboo shoots and pork into fine shreds. Shell and de-vein the shrimps, and chop into small pieces. Heat the peanut oil in a wok, or frying pan, and sauté the shrimps, pork and vegetables for 2 minutes. Add the Chinese wine, soya sauce, sugar, salt, pepper, monosodium glutamate and 25 ml. of cold water, and stir over high heat for a further 2 minutes. Mix the cornstarch with a little cold water, and add to the pan to thicken the mixture. Remove pan from the heat and allow mixture to cool. Place the wrappers on a flat lightly greased surface, and spoon equal portions of the mixture on to each. Roll up the wrappers diagonally, tuck in the ends, and seal with the beaten egg. Heat the vegetable oil in a wok, or deep pan, and fry the spring rolls until golden brown in colour.

'Dim Sum Selections' prepared for photography by **Lo Fung Restaurant**, The Peak.

Rice & Noodles
麵飯

Rice or noodles are a staple of nearly all Chinese diets, and as such will be seen, in one form or another, at every table. Often they are served as a side dish to the main courses, but they also can be used to make very filling and flavourful main dishes, such as the Special Fried Rice and Noodles in Soup included in this section. In particular, noodles of all shapes and sizes can be cooked in a wide variety of ways, and often, outside the home, some of the most tasty dishes can be found in the small and unpretentious street stalls.

'Rice and Noodles' prepared for photography by **Jade Garden Restaurant**, Star House, Kowloon.

Boiled Rice

200 g long grained rice
800 ml water (approximately)
¼ teaspoon salt

First wash the rice under cold running water, then drain thoroughly. Place into a saucepan, and pour in sufficient cold water to come to a depth of $\frac{1}{2}$ inch above the level of rice. Add the salt, and bring to the boil. Allow to boil rapidly for 1 minute, then lower heat and simmer until all the water has been absorbed, approximately 6 minutes. Bring 300 ml. of water to the boil, and pour over the rice. Place a tightly fitting lid on the pan, and simmer over low heat for 3-4 minutes, then remove from the heat, and let stand, still tightly covered for a further 5 minutes. (During this time the rice will continue to cook in its own heat.) Remove the lid to make sure the rice is by now dry and fluffy, if not re-cover, and leave for a little longer.

Steamed Rice

200 g long grained rice
400 ml water (approximately)
¼ teaspoon salt
1 teaspoon peanut oil

First wash the rice under cold running water, and drain thoroughly. Place into a saucepan, and add just sufficient cold water to cover the rice. Add the salt, bring to the boil, and allow to simmer gently for 3-4 minutes. Remove and drain. Place the rice in a large bowl, or individual rice bowls, if preferred, sprinkle over the peanut oil, and place in a tightly sealed container. Steam until the rice is fluffy, approximately $1\frac{1}{4}$ hours.

Special Fried Rice

200 g long grained rice
½ teaspoon salt
50 g fresh shrimps
50 g pork
50 g chicken meat
½ cabbage
2 spring onions
1 brown onion
2 eggs
¼ teaspoon white pepper
50 ml vegetable oil
25 g cooked green peas
1 tablespoon light soya sauce

Boil the rice (see recipe opposite) using half the salt. Leave in the covered pan to keep warm, until required, but be sure not to overcook. Shell and de-vein the shrimps, and cut into halves, lengthways. Chop the pork and chicken meat into small cubes. Shred the cabbage, and chop the spring onions and brown onion. Beat the eggs in a bowl, and add the white pepper and the remaining salt. Heat the oil in a wok, or large frying pan, add the pork, and stir fry for 2 minutes, then add the shrimps, shredded cabbage and onions. Continue to cook over medium heat for a further 2 minutes, stirring frequently, then remove everything to the side of the pan. Pour the beaten egg into the centre of the pan, and when it begins to set, break up with a fork, and mix in with the other ingredients. Then add the cooked peas, the soya sauce and the boiled rice. Mix well and continue to stir-fry for 3-4 minutes.

* Note: According to taste, the above recipe may be varied many ways. Beef, for example, may be used, or the dish can be prepared with different seafoods, or as a vegetarian dish.

Vegetarian Noodles

100 g noodles
½ teaspoon salt
4 dried Chinese mushrooms
50 g bean sprouts
1 green pepper
2 carrots
1 inch knob fresh ginger
500 ml vegetable oil
25 g cooked peas
25 ml Chinese wine
2 teaspoons light soya sauce
1 teaspoon dark soya sauce
2 teaspoons cornstarch
1 teaspoon sesame oil

Cover the noodles with cold water, add the salt, bring to the boil, and let simmer for 6-7 minutes. Remove, and drain thoroughly. Heat the oil in a wok, or large pan, and deep fry the noodles for 2-3 minutes. Remove, drain off all excess oil, arrange in a serving dish, and keep warm. Soak the mushrooms in warm water for 30 minutes, remove and discard the hard stems, and cut into shreds. Immerse the bean sprouts in boiling water for 1 minute, then remove and drain. Chop green pepper and carrots, and cut the ginger into thin slices. Heat the oil in a wok, or large pan, and deep fry the noodles for 2-3 minutes. Remove, drain off all excess oil, arrange in a serving dish, and keep warm. Pour off most of the oil from the pan, and add the mushrooms, bean sprouts, green pepper, carrots and ginger, and stir-fry over medium heat for 2 minutes. Add the cooked peas, Chinese wine, soya sauce and 50 ml. of cold water, and let simmer for a further 2 minutes. Mix the cornstarch with a small quantity of cold water, and add to the pan. Stir to blend well, and to allow the sauce to thicken slightly, then pour over the noodles. Finally, heat the sesame oil, and sprinkle over the noodles.

Szechuan Noodles

150 g noodles
6 dried Chinese mushrooms
100 g fresh prawns
100 g fresh abalone
½ Chinese cabbage
100 g cooked chicken meat
100 g cooked ham
25 ml peanut oil
1 tablespoon chilli sauce
½ tablespoon dark soya sauce
½ teaspoon salt
1 tablespoon cornstarch
1 egg

Bring a pan of water to the boil, and cook the noodles for 5 minutes. Drain and set aside. Soak the mushrooms in warm water for 30 minutes, remove and discard the hard stems, and cut into halves. Shell and de-vein the prawns, and cut into half lengthways. Cut the abalone into thin slices, shred the cabbage, and cut the chicken meat and ham into small dice. Heat the oil in a wok, or frying pan, and fry the noodles until golden. Drain off the oil, and add the mushrooms, cabbage, prawns and abalone. Stir-fry for 2 minutes, then add the chicken meat, ham, chilli sauce, soya sauce and salt, and continue to stir for a further 30 seconds. Mix the cornstarch with a small quantity of cold water and add to the noodles, then heat the sesame oil, and stir in. Finally after arranging on a serving dish, fry the egg, and place on top of the noodles.

Noodles in Soup

150 g noodles
1 teaspoon salt
4 dried Chinese mushrooms
2 fresh red chillies
2 small red onions
75 g fresh pork
25 ml vegetable oil
800 ml chicken stock
25 ml Chinese wine
1 teaspoon dark soya sauce
¼ teaspoon white pepper
dash monosodium glutamate
2 spring onions

In a saucepan, cover the noodles with cold water, add half the salt, and bring to the boil. Simmer for 10 minutes, then remove and wash under cold running water. Return noodles to the pan, bring water back to the boil, then drain noodles thoroughly, place in a soup tureen, and keep warm. Soak the mushrooms in warm water for 30 minutes, and discard the hard stems. Cut the chillies into shreds, and slice the red onions. Shred the pork meat. Heat the oil in a wok, or large saucepan, and sauté the pork, for 1 minute. Remove and drain, and pour off most of the oil from the pan. Add the stock to the pan, and bring to the boil. Then put back the pork, and add the mushrooms, chillies, red onions, Chinese wine, soya sauce, pepper, monosodium glutamate and remaining salt. Simmer for 5-6 minutes, then pour over the noodles. Cut the spring onions into 1 inch lengths, and float on top of the soup.

Soups
湯類

Soup is an important part of a Chinese meal, and is nearly always served at home and in a restaurant. At more formal dinners or banquets, soup will be served twice. A thick and substantial soup will be served halfway through the meal, and a light clear soup towards the end, to clear the palate for the sweet course to follow. Vegetables, fish, chicken and meat all go to make up a variety of nourishing and tasty soups. Two of the most popular ingredients for special soups, which are not used in Western cooking, but which are both readily available in dried form, are Shark's Fin and Bird's Nest.

Fresh Fish Head Soup

150 g fresh fish head
1 inch knob fresh ginger
100 g bamboo shoots
1 tablespoon vinegar
25 ml Chinese wine
¼ teaspoon white pepper
½ teaspoon salt
2 fresh red chillies
2 fresh green chillies
25 ml vegetable oil
1 litre fish stock
25 ml dark soya sauce

Scale and thoroughly wash the fish head, cut into 2 inch pieces and place into a shallow dish. Finely chop the ginger and bamboo shoots and place in the dish with the fish head. Pour over the vinegar and Chinese wine, season with the pepper and salt, and allow to stand for 30 minutes. Chop the chillies. Heat the oil in a large deep pan, sauté the chillies for 1 minute, then add the fish head and all the marinade, and keep over medium heat for 5 minutes, stirring continuously. Bring the stock to the boil, pour over the fish head, add the soya sauce, cover, and simmer for a further 5 minutes.

Seafood and Beancurd Soup

150 g small fish fillets
50 g fresh prawns
½ teaspoon salt
¼ teaspoon white pepper
dash monosodium glutamate
3 dried Chinese mushrooms
2 spring onions
½ inch knob fresh ginger
1 clove garlic
150 g bean curd
50 ml vegetable oil
1 tablespoon Chinese wine
750 ml fish stock
2 teaspoons light soya sauce
1 teaspoon dark soya sauce
1 teaspoon chopped parsley

Remove any skin from the fish, and shell and de-vein the prawns. Season with salt, pepper and monosodium glutamate, and allow to stand for 30 minutes. Soak the mushrooms in warm water for 30 minutes, remove and discard the hard stems, and cut into thin shreds. Chop the spring onions, crush the ginger and garlic, and cut the beancurd into 1 inch squares. Heat the oil in a wok, or small pan, and fry the fish for 1 minute. Add the prawns, and continue over medium heat for a further minute. Remove the seafood from the wok and place into a large saucepan. Sprinkle over the wine and pour in the stock. Bring to the boil, add the mushrooms, onions, ginger, garlic, bean curd and soya sauce, and simmer for 10 minutes. Pour into a tureen, and sprinkle on the chopped parsley.

Sour Pepper Soup

3 dried Chinese mushrooms
40 g bamboo shoots
50 g beancurd
3 spring onions
50 g lean cooked pork
30 g cooked shrimps, shelled
25 ml peanut oil
1 teaspoon white pepper
1 tablespoon vinegar
½ tablespoon dark soya sauce
½ teaspoon salt
½ teaspoon sesame oil
1 litre chicken stock
2 tablespoons cornstarch
1 egg

Soak the mushrooms in warm water for 30 minutes, and discard the hard stems. Chop the mushrooms, bamboo shoots and spring onions, and cut the beancurd into small dice. Shred the pork and finely chop the shrimps. Heat the peanut oil in a small pan, add the chopped onion, pepper, vinegar, soya sauce, salt and sesame oil, and cook gently for 1 minute. Cover and keep hot. In another pan, bring the stock to the boil, add the mushroom, bamboo shoots, beancurd, pork and shrimps, and simmer gently for 2 minutes. Mix the cornstarch with a little cold water and add to the stock, then break in the egg, and simmer for a further minute, stirring continuously. To serve place a small quantity of the hot and sour onion mixture into individual bowls and pour over the soup. Garnish with chopped spring onion.

Chinese Mushroom and Egg Soup

10 dried Chinese mushrooms
1 litre chicken stock
3 eggs
¼ teaspoon white pepper
salt to taste
1 spring onion
1 sprig parsley

Soak the mushrooms in warm water for 30 minutes, remove and discard the hard stems, and cut into strips. Place in a large deep pan, pour in the stock and bring slowly to the boil. When the stock is simmering gently, break in the eggs one by one and stir briskly. Season with the pepper and salt to taste and continue to simmer for a further 10 minutes. Pour into a serving bowl and add the freshly chopped spring onion and parsley.

Soups prepared for photography by **Lychee Village Restaurant**, Kowloon.
('Fresh Fish Head Soup', Page 21; 'Chinese Mushroom and Egg', Page 22; 'Pig's Liver and Tomato Soup', Page 29.)

Mushroom and Crispy Rice Soup

8 dried Chinese mushrooms
200 g sticky rice
1 litre chicken stock
½ teaspoon salt
¼ teaspoon white pepper
1 teaspoon dark soya sauce
1 tablespoon Chinese wine
400 ml vegetable oil
1 teaspoon chopped parsley

Place the mushrooms in a shallow dish, and add just sufficient warm water to cover them. Allow to stand for 30 minutes, after which time, remove and discard the hard stems, but retain the water. Steam the rice in a large pan, until it is overcooked, and sticks to the bottom of the pan. Remove carefully, and cut into pieces. Next bring the stock to the boil, add the mushrooms and the reserved water, season with the salt, pepper, soya sauce and Chinese wine, and simmer gently for 20-25 minutes. Heat the oil in a wok, or large pan, and deep fry the pieces of rice until they are crispy and golden. Pour the boiling stock into a tureen, and immediately add the crispy rice, which should make a sizzling sound. Finally sprinkle on the chopped parsley.

'Mushroom and Crispy Rice Soup' prepared for photography by **Peking Garden Restaurant**, Causeway Bay.

Shark's Fin and Chicken Soup

150 g dried shark's fin
75 g cooked chicken meat
2 spring onions
1 inch knob fresh ginger
25 ml peanut oil
1 tablespoon Chinese wine
400 ml chicken stock
2 teaspoons cornstarch
½ teaspoon dark soya sauce
salt to taste
freshly ground black pepper
1 tablespoon chopped ham

Soak the shark's fin in cold water for at least 12 hours. Drain, cover with fresh water, bring to the boil, and allow to simmer for 30 minutes. Remove and drain thoroughly. Cut the chicken meat into thin shreds, and chop finely the spring onions and ginger. Heat the oil in a wok, or large pan, and sauté the onions and ginger for 1 minute. Add the shark's fin, Chinese wine and stock, bring to the boil, then simmer for 30 minutes. Add the chicken, stir well, and continue to simmer for a further 2 minutes. Mix the cornstarch with a small quantity of cold water and add to the pan. Add the soya sauce, salt, freshly ground black pepper to taste, and pour into a tureen. Sprinkle the chopped ham on top.

Chicken and Sweet Corn Soup

1 chicken breast
1 egg white
½ teaspoon salt
¼ teaspoon white pepper
dash monosodium glutamate
800 ml clear chicken stock
200 g sweet corn
1 tablespoon Chinese wine
½ tablespoon light soya sauce
1 teaspoon dark soya sauce
1 teaspoon sesame oil
1 tablespoon cornstarch
1 tablespoon shredded cooked ham

De-bone the chicken, and chop the meat very finely. Beat the egg white, season with the salt, pepper and monosodium glutamate, pour over the chicken, and allow to marinate for 20 minutes. Bring the stock to the boil, add the corn, Chinese wine, soya sauce and sesame oil, and simmer for 3 minutes. Add the chicken and the marinade, and continue to simmer for a further 2-3 minutes. Mix the cornstarch with a small quantity of cold water, and stir into the soup to thicken. Pour the soup into a tureen, and sprinkle over the shredded ham.

Shredded Chicken and Crabmeat Soup

1 chicken breast
¼ teaspoon salt
freshly ground black pepper
800 ml chicken stock
2 spring onions
50 g button mushrooms
25 ml Chinese wine
1 tablespoon light soya sauce
dash monosodium glutamate
150 g cooked crabmeat
1 teaspoon chopped parsley

Season the chicken breast with the salt and freshly ground black pepper. Cover with the stock, bring to the boil, and allow to simmer gently for 25 minutes. Take out the breast, remove all the meat from the bone, and cut into shreds. Chop the spring onions, and add to the stock, together with the mushrooms, Chinese wine, soya sauce and monosodium glutamate. Simmer for a further 5 minutes, add the crabmeat and chicken, stir to heat through thoroughly, then pour into a tureen, and sprinkle over the chopped parsley.

Bird's Nest with Quail Egg Soup

50 g dried bird's nest
1 tablespoon Chinese wine
1 litre chicken stock
50 g snow peas
2 spring onions
½ teaspoon salt
¼ teaspoon white pepper
dash monosodium glutamate
12 quail eggs
1 tablespoon shredded ham

Soak bird's nest in water for 4·hours. Remove any feathers or impurities, and place into a pan. Cover with 100 ml. of cold water, and bring to the boil. Lower heat, add the Chinese wine, and allow to simmer for 30 minutes. Drain and set aside. Bring the chicken stock to the boil, add the snow peas and the spring onions cut into 1 inch lengths, and season with the salt, pepper and monosodium glutamate. Allow to simmer for 5 minutes, then add bird's nest, and continue over medium heat for a further 2-3 minutes. Break the eggs into small dishes, sprinkle on top the shredded ham, and poach for 2-3 minutes. To serve pour the soup into a tureen, and float the poached quail eggs on top.

Bird's Nest and Chicken Soup

40 g birds' nest
100 g cooked chicken meat
3 egg whites
1 litre chicken stock
dash monosodium glutamate
¼ teaspoon white pepper
salt to taste
½ tablespoon light soya sauce
1 tablespoon cornstarch
2 tablespoons cooked diced ham

Soak the bird's nest in cold water for 5-6 hours. Remove any impurities, rinse thoroughly, and allow to drain. Place in a tightly sealed container, and steam for 1 hour. Mince the chicken meat, beat the eggs, and mix together to form a thick paste. In a large saucepan bring the stock to the boil, season with monosodium glutamate, pepper, salt and soya sauce, and simmer gently for 15 minutes. Mix the cornstarch with a little cold water, and add the stock together with the chicken paste. Stir until the soup thickens. To serve place a small quantity of steamed bird's nest into individual bowls, pour in the soup, and sprinkle over a little diced ham.

Pig's Liver and Tomato Soup

180 g pig's liver
1 spring onion
1 inch knob fresh ginger
1 tablespoon sugar
¼ teaspoon white pepper
salt to taste
1 tablespoon dark soya sauce
25 ml vegetable oil
1 litre chicken stock
150 g fresh tomatoes

Slice the liver into 1 inch pieces, and place into a shallow dish. Chop the spring onion and ginger, and place in the dish with the liver. Add the sugar, pepper, salt to taste and the soya sauce, and allow to stand for 30 minutes. Heat the oil in a wok, or frying pan, add the liver and marinade ingredients, and stir-fry for 5 minutes over a medium heat. In a large pan bring the stock to the boil, and when simmering add the liver. Slice the tomatoes, place into the wok and cook for 2-3 minutes. Transfer all the ingredients from the wok into the stock, cover, and simmer over low heat for a further 5 minutes.

Shredded Beef and Egg Soup

150 g lean beef
½ teaspoon salt
freshly ground black pepper
1 teaspoon cornstarch
½ teaspoon baking soda
1 tablespoon light soya sauce
25 ml peanut oil
½ teaspoon sesame oil
500 ml stock
3 egg whites
2 spring onions
1 sprig parsley

Shred the beef, and season with the salt and freshly ground pepper. Mix the cornstarch, baking soda, soya sauce and peanut oil, and pour over the beef. Sprinkle on the sesame oil, and allow to marinate for 20 minutes. Remove the beef, and strain. Retain the marinade juices. In a large saucepan bring some water to the boil, add the beef, and boil rapidly for 3 minutes, stirring continuously. Pour off the water, and add the stock to the pan. Bring back to the boil, and allow to simmer for 10 minutes, then pour in the reserved marinade and continue to simmer for a further 5 minutes. Lightly beat the egg whites, and gradually stir into the soup. Pour into a tureen, chop the spring onions and parsley, and sprinkle on top.

Seafoods

海鮮

The waters around Hong Kong abound with a wide variety of seafood, and the picturesque junks can be seen, each and every day of the year, bringing in fresh supplies. To the Chinese cook, professional chef or housewife, 'fresh' is all-important. Fish is often taken home from the market in a plastic bag of water, and only killed immediately prior to cooking, and when eating out, many of the excellent seafood restaurants, which are to be found everywhere, offer the opportunity of selecting the fish of one's choice directly from the live-fish tank. In addition to being the primary ingredient in an incredible number of tasty and colourful dishes, many seafoods, such as shrimps, oysters and squid, are used to add different textures and flavours to meat and poultry.

Lobster with Chinese Wine and Tomato Sauce

1 fresh lobster, about 1 kilo
½ teaspoon salt
freshly ground black pepper
500 ml vegetable oil
250 ml fish stock
25 ml Chinese wine
25 ml tomato sauce
2 teaspoons sugar
dash monosodium glutamate
1 tablespoon cornstarch

Place the lobster in rapidly boiling water until it turns red. Remove and discard the head and tail, and chop the body into approximately 16 pieces. (Note: Do not remove the meat from the shell.) Season the lobster with the salt and freshly ground black pepper. Heat the oil in a wok, or deep pan, until almost smoking, and deep-fry the lobster pieces for 30 seconds. Remove and set aside to drain, and pour off most of the oil from the pan. Pour the stock into the pan, and bring to the boil. Add the Chinese wine, tomato sauce, sugar and monosodium glutamate, and blend thoroughly. Mix the cornstarch with a little cold water and add to the sauce. Finally return the lobster pieces to the pan, and simmer over a low heat for 2-3 minutes.

Lobster with Soya Beans and Green Pepper

1 fresh lobster, about 1 kilo
½ teaspoon salt
¼ teaspoon white pepper
1 tablespoon cornstarch
1 green pepper
1 clove garlic
½ tablespoon fermented soya
  beans
150 ml peanut oil
25 ml Chinese wine
1 teaspoon light soya sauce
1 teaspoon sugar
dash monosodium glutamate
125 ml fish stock

Place the lobster in rapidly boiling water until it turns red. Remove all the meat, cut into cubes, season with salt and pepper, and sprinkle with half the cornstarch. Cut off the head and tail, and arrange on a warm serving platter. Wash the green pepper, discard the seeds, and cut into pieces. Crush the garlic and soya beans. Heat the oil in a wok, or deep pan, and fry the lobster for 30 seconds. Remove and drain. Add the green pepper to the pan, fry for 2 minutes, then remove and drain. Arrange the lobster and pepper on the serving platter, between the head and tail, and set aside in a warm place. Pour away most of the oil from the pan, and add the garlic and fermented soya beans. Sauté for 15 seconds, then add the Chinese wine, soya sauce, sugar and monosodium glutamate. Mix the remaining cornstarch with the cold stock, and add to the pan. Bring to the boil, allow to simmer gently for 2-3 minutes, then pour over the lobster.

'Lobster with Soya Beans and Green Pepper' prepared for photography by **Man Wah Restaurant**, Mandarin Hotel.

Sweet and Sour Prawns

400 g fresh prawns
1 egg
25 g sugar
25 ml vinegar
1 tablespoon light soya sauce
1 tablespoon tomato sauce
25 g cornstarch
1 large brown onion
2 spring onions
2 fresh red chillies
1 green pepper
½ inch knob fresh ginger
1 clove garlic
50 ml vegetable oil
50 g canned pineapple chunks

Shell and de-vein the prawns. Wash in cold water, dry thoroughly, and place in a shallow dish. Beat the egg, add the sugar, vinegar, soya sauce and tomato sauce, and pour over the prawns. Allow the prawns to marinate for 15 minutes, then remove and dust with the cornstarch. Slice the brown onion, chop the spring onions, chillies, green pepper and ginger, and crush the garlic. Heat the oil in a wok, or large pan, add the prawns, and stir-fry for 2-3 minutes. Remove the prawns, drain, and set aside in a warming oven. Pour off most of the oil from the pan, add the slices of brown onion, and sauté for 2-3 minutes, until golden brown. Then add the spring onions, chillies, green pepper, ginger and garlic, and continue to stir, over medium heat, for a further 3 minutes. Finally put back the prawns, add the pineapple chunks, mix together well, and allow to heat through.

'Sweet and Sour Prawns' prepared for photography by **Golden Lotus Restaurant**, Hongkong Hilton Hotel.

Prawn Cutlets

8 king size prawns
1 egg
½ teaspoon salt
freshly ground black pepper
dash monosodium glutamate
1 tablespoon Chinese wine
1 teaspoon light soya sauce
1 teaspoon dark soya sauce
1 tablespoon cornstarch
500 ml vegetable oil

Shell and de-vein the prawns, cut into halves, lengthways, and fold out to flatten. Beat the egg, add the Chinese wine, and season with the salt, freshly ground black pepper, monosodium glutamate and soya sauce. Marinate the prawn cutlets in the seasoned egg for 15 minutes, then remove and coat with the cornstarch. Heat the oil in a wok, or large pan, until almost smoking, and deep fry the prawns for 2-3 minutes. Remove and drain off all excess oil.

Steamed Prawns with Garlic and Black Beans

300 g fresh prawns
2 cloves garlic
1 fresh red chilli
2 spring onions
1 tablespoon fermented black beans
1 teaspoon sugar
½ teaspoon salt
¼ teaspoon white pepper
dash monosodium glutamate
25 ml Chinese wine

Wash the prawns, remove the heads, but leave the remaining shell intact. Crush the garlic, and chop finely the chilli and spring onions. Place the prawns in a shallow heatproof dish, and cover evenly with the garlic, chilli, onion and black beans. Season with the sugar, salt, pepper and monosodium glutamate, and pour over the Chinese wine. Place the dish in a tightly sealed container, and steam for 8 minutes.

Shrimps with Green Peas

500 g fresh shrimps
2 spring onions
½ inch knob fresh ginger
2 cloves garlic
25 ml vegetable oil
100 g cooked green peas
75 ml fish or chicken stock
¼ teaspoon white pepper
dash monosodium glutamate
2 teaspoons light soya sauce
1 teaspoon sugar
1 teaspoon sesame oil

Shell and de-vein the shrimps, then wash and dry thoroughly. Chop the spring onions, ginger and garlic. Heat the oil in a wok, or frying pan, and saute the shrimps, onions, ginger and garlic for 2-3 minutes. Remove and set aside, then add peas to the pan, and stir for 1 minute. Pour in the stock, replace the shrimps and vegetables, and season with the pepper, monosodium glutamate, soya sauce and sugar. Bring to the boil, and allow to simmer gently for a further 2 minutes. Heat the sesame oil, and sprinkle over just prior to serving.

Fried Shrimps with Walnuts

180 g fresh shrimps
125 g walnuts
3 spring onions
4 carrots
1 inch knob fresh ginger
30 g vegetable oil
¼ teaspoon white pepper
salt to taste

Shell and de-vein the shrimps, and shell the walnuts. Cut the spring onions into 2 inch lengths, slice the carrots and finely chop the ginger. Heat half the oil in a wok, or frying pan, and stir-fry the walnuts for 2 minutes. Pour in the remaining oil, and add the shrimps. Continue to cook over medium heat for 3 minutes, before adding the onions, carrots and ginger. Finally season with pepper and salt to taste, and stir-fry for a further 2-3 minutes.

Shrimps in Hot Garlic Sauce

400 g fresh shrimps
1 egg white
25 ml Chinese wine
1 tablespoon cornstarch
½ teaspoon salt
1 brown onion
2 spring onions
3 fresh red chillies
½ inch knob fresh ginger
2 cloves garlic
400 ml vegetable oil
125 ml fish stock
1 tablespoon black bean paste
1 tablespoon light soya sauce
1 teaspoon sugar
1 teaspoon sesame oil

Shell, wash and de-vein the shrimps, and cut in half length-wise. Lightly beat the egg white, add the wine, half the cornstarch and the salt, and mix well. Add the shrimps and allow to marinate for 30 minutes. Finely chop the brown onion, spring onions, chillies, ginger and garlic. Heat the oil in a wok, or deep pan, spoon in the coated shrimps, and fry for about 2 minutes, until the shrimps turn pink. Remove, drain thoroughly and set aside in a warm place. Pour off most of the oil, add the onions, chillies, ginger and garlic, and place over moderate heat for 5 minutes, stirring continuously. Then add the stock, bean paste, soya sauce and sugar, and bring back to the boil. Replace the shrimps, lower the heat, and allow to gently simmer for a further 2-3 minutes. Mix the remaining cornstarch with a little cold water, then add to the pan and stir well until the sauce thickens. After arranging in a serving dish sprinkle with the sesame oil.

Cuttlefish with Bean Sprouts

300 g small cuttlefish
2 spring onions
1 green pepper
2 carrots
1 clove garlic
50 ml peanut oil
100 g bean sprouts
1 tablespoon light soya sauce
1 tablespoon oyster sauce
¼ teaspoon white pepper
1 teaspoon sugar
1 teaspoon sesame oil

Clean the cuttlefish thoroughly, discarding the ink-sac and head section. Cover with cold water and allow to stand for 30 minutes. Remove and drain, then put into a pan of fresh water, bring to the boil, and cook for 2-3 minutes. Remove and dry thoroughly. Chop the spring onions, green pepper and carrots into small pieces, and crush the garlic. Heat the oil in a wok, or frying pan, add the chopped vegetables and garlic, and sauté for 1 minute. Add the cuttlefish, and stir-fry over high heat for 3 minutes, then add the bean sprouts, soya sauce, oyster sauce, pepper and sugar. Cook for a further 2 minutes, and just prior to serving add the hot sesame oil.

Sautéed Squid with Minced Pork

100 g fresh squid
50 ml vegetable oil
100 g lean pork
2 spring onions
1 clove garlic
½ teaspoon salt
¼ teaspoon white pepper
1 teaspoon light soya sauce
1 teaspoon dark soya sauce
1 teaspoon oyster sauce

Clean the squid, and carefully remove and discard the ink-sac. Heat the oil in a wok, or frying pan, and sauté the squid for 1 minute, then remove and chop into very small pieces. Mince the pork, finely chop the spring onions, and crush the garlic. Mix together the squid, pork, spring onions and garlic, and season with the salt, white pepper and soya sauce. Re-heat the oil in the pan, add the mixture, and stir-fry over high heat for 2-3 minutes. Finally add the oyster sauce, and continue to stir for a further 30 seconds.

Crabmeat Omelette

300 g crabmeat
½ teaspoon salt
¼ teaspoon white pepper
2 spring onions
½ inch knob fresh ginger
1 clove garlic
1 small green pepper
25 ml peanut oil
1 tablespoon Chinese wine
6 eggs
1 teaspoon chopped chives *
1 teaspoon sesame oil
2 teaspoons light soya sauce

Flake the crabmeat, and season with the salt and white pepper. Chop the spring onions and green pepper into very small pieces, and crush the ginger and garlic. Heat half the peanut oil in a wok, or frying pan, add the crabmeat, onion, pepper, ginger, garlic and Chinese wine, and stir-fry for 1 minute. Remove and clean the pan. Break the eggs into a bowl, mix lightly with a fork, and add the chives, sesame oil, soya sauce and crabmeat mixture. Heat the remaining oil in the wok, swirl around to make certain the complete cooking surface is greased, then pour in a quarter of the omelette mixture. Cook over a low heat, turning once. Remove, keep warm, and cook the remaining mixture in a similar manner.
* Note: Depending on taste, chopped parsley may be substituted for chives.

Steamed Crab with Ginger and Spring Onions

1 fresh crab, about 400 g
½ teaspoon salt
freshly ground black pepper
½ inch knob fresh ginger
2 spring onions
1 egg
25 ml Chinese wine
½ teaspoon crushed garlic
1 tablespoon peanut oil

Place the crab in rapidly boiling water for 2-3 minutes. Remove the claws and top shell, chop the body of the crab into approximately 6 pieces, season with the salt and freshly ground black pepper, and arrange in a shallow heat-proof dish. Chop the ginger and spring onions, and sprinkle over the crab pieces. Beat the egg, mix with the Chinese wine and the crushed garlic, and pour over the crab. Finally pour on the peanut oil, place the dish in a sealed container, and cook over boiling water for 10-15 minutes.

Baked Stuffed Crab Shell

1 fresh crab, about 500 g
1 egg
½ teaspoon salt
¼ teaspoon white pepper
2 dried Chinese mushrooms
3 fresh prawns
25 g chicken livers
1 brown onion
25 ml vegetable oil
25 ml fish or chicken stock
1 tablespoon light soya sauce
½ tablespoon cornstarch
1 tablespoon breadcrumbs

Cook the crab in rapidly boiling water for 4-5 minutes. Remove the top shell carefully, clean and place in a warming oven. Extract all the meat from the body and claws of the crab, and place into a shallow dish. Beat the egg and pour over the crabmeat. Season with the salt and pepper, and allow to stand for 30 minutes. Soak the mushrooms in warm water for 30 minutes, remove and discard the hard stems, and chop into small pieces. Shell the prawns, and chop into small pieces. Also chop the chicken livers and onion. Heat the oil in a wok, or frying pan, and sauté the onion until golden in colour, then add the crabmeat, mushrooms, prawns and chicken livers. Continue to cook over a moderate heat for 2 minutes, stirring to mix thoroughly. Add the stock, the soya sauce, and the cornstarch mixed with a little cold water. Cook for a further minute, then spoon into the warmed shell. Sprinkle over the breadcrumbs, and cook in a moderate oven for approximately 10 minutes, until the top is golden.

Deep Fried Crab Claws

8 crab claws
150 g fresh shrimps
50 g fat pork
1 teaspoon sugar
dash monosodium glutamate
¼ teaspoon white pepper
salt to taste
1 teaspoon light soya sauce
1 teaspoon dark soya sauce
1 teaspoon sesame oil
1 egg white
2 tablespoons cornstarch
500 ml vegetable oil

Boil the crab claws in salted water for 10 minutes. Carefully crack the crab claws and remove the shells, leaving each crab claw meat intact and attached to the nipper end. Mince the shrimps and the fat pork, and add the sugar, monosodium glutamate, pepper, salt, soya sauce and sesame oil. Beat the egg into the mixture, add half the cornstarch, and blend thoroughly. Mould the mixture around the crab claw meat, and roll in the remaining cornstarch. Heat the oil in a wok, or large pan, and deep fry until golden. Allow to drain, then serve immediately.

'Deep Fried Crab Claws' prepared for photography by **Miramar Theatre Restaurant**, Miramar Hotel.

Crab with Pork and Egg

2 fresh crabs, about 400 g each
4 thin slices cooked pork
3 spring onions
3 small red onions
1 inch knob fresh ginger
2 cloves garlic
4 eggs
1 tablespoon fermented black beans
1 tablespoon shredded dried
   orange peel
1 tablespoon Chinese wine
1 tablespoon light soya sauce
freshly ground black pepper
dash monosodium glutamate
2 teaspoons sesame oil

Cook the crabs in rapidly boiling, salted, water for 5 minutes. Carefully remove the top shells, clean, and set aside. Crack the claws, and extract all the crab meat. Place the crab meat on a heatproof dish, and cover with the slices of pork. Chop the spring onions, red onions and ginger, and crush the garlic. Heat the eggs in a mixing bowl, and add the onions, ginger, garlic, black beans and dried orange peel. Combine thoroughly, then add the Chinese wine, soya sauce, freshly ground black pepper and monosodium glutamate. Spread the mixture evenly over the crab and pork, place the dish in a tightly sealed container, and steam for 20 minutes. Remove from the steamer, place ingredients in a casserole, pour over the sesame oil, and cook in a pre-heated medium oven for a further 10 minutes. Serve in the warmed crab shells.

'Crab with Pork and Egg' prepared for photography by **Riverside Restaurant**, Causeway Bay.

Deep Fried Scallops with Chicken Livers

12 fresh scallops
150 g chicken livers
2 spring onions
2 small red onions
1 inch knob fresh ginger
1 clove garlic
1 egg
1 tablespoon Chinese wine
25 ml fish stock
½ teaspoon salt
¼ teaspoon white pepper
dash monosodium glutamate
500 ml vegetable oil
2 teaspoons cornstarch

Wash the scallops, trim off any ragged edges, and cut each scallop into three pieces. Wash the chicken livers, cut into halves, and immerse into boiling water for 30 seconds. Chop the spring onions, red onions and ginger into very small pieces, and crush the garlic. Beat the egg lightly, add the onions, ginger, garlic, Chinese wine, stock, salt, white pepper and monosodium glutamate, and combine thoroughly. Place the pieces of scallop and liver into the mixture, and leave to marinate for 20 minutes. Remove and place the scallops and livers into a wire frying basket. Retain the marinade. Heat the oil in a deep pan, and fry the scallops and livers for approximately 1 minute. Remove and set aside. Pour off all but about 25 ml. of the oil, add the marinade to the pan, and simmer gently for 1 minute. Mix the cornstarch with a small quantity of cold water, and add to the pan. Finally add the scallops and chicken livers, and continue to cook over low heat for a further 2 minutes.

Braised Abalone with Celery and Onions

250 g canned boiled abalone
50 g lard
1 teaspoon sugar
½ teaspoon salt
2 sticks celery
2 spring onions
1 tablespoon Chinese wine
1 tablespoon light soya sauce
1 teaspoon dark soya sauce
25 ml chicken stock
freshly ground black pepper
dash monosodium glutamate
1 teaspoon cornstarch
25 ml oyster sauce

Drain the abalone, wash under running water, and dry thoroughly. Heat half the quantity of lard in a wok, or saucepan, add the abalone, sugar, and salt, cover the pan, and cook over very low heat for 30 minutes. Remove the abalone, and cut into fine shreds. Chop the celery and spring onions into fairly small pieces. In a clean wok, or pan, heat the remaining lard, add the abalone, and sauté for 1 minute. Then add the celery, spring onions, Chinese wine, soya sauce, stock, freshly ground black pepper and monosodium glutamate, and stir over medium heat for 3-4 minutes. Mix the cornstarch with a small quantity of cold water, and add to the pan. Finally pour in the oyster sauce, stir to mix in thoroughly, and allow to simmer for a further minute.

Frogs Legs with Pepper and Hot Garlic Sauce

200 g frogs legs
freshly ground black pepper
4 sticks celery
50 ml vegetable oil
2 cloves garlic
3 spring onions
½ inch knob fresh ginger
½ tablespoon sugar
½ tablespoon light soya sauce
1 teaspoon dark soya sauce
½ tablespoon chilli sauce
25 ml Chinese wine
1 tablespoon cornstarch
½ tablespoon vinegar

Wash the frogs legs and dry thoroughly. Cut into halves, and season with freshly ground black pepper. Cut the celery into 2 inch lengths. Heat the oil in a wok, or frying pan, and sauté the frogs legs and celery for 5 minutes, stirring occasionally. Remove from the pan, and set aside in a warm place. Crush the garlic, finely chop the spring onions and ginger and add to the pan. Stir over medium heat for 30 seconds, then add the sugar, soya sauce, chilli sauce and Chinese wine. Stir for a further 30 seconds, then add 50 ml. of cold water. Bring back to the boil, and replace the frogs legs and celery. Allow to simmer gently for 1 minute, then thicken with the cornstarch mixed with a little cold water. Just prior to serving stir in the vinegar.

Sautéed Frogs Legs with Chillies and Sesame Oil

250 g frogs legs
½ tablespoon cornstarch
25 ml Chinese wine
½ teaspoon salt
¼ teaspoon white pepper
75 ml vegetable oil
3 fresh red chillies
4 spring onions
1 teaspoon sugar
1 tablespoon light soya sauce
1 tablespoon sesame oil

Wash and thoroughly dry the frogs legs, and chop into small pieces. Sprinkle over the cornstarch and the Chinese wine, season with salt and pepper, and allow to stand for 10 minutes. Heat the oil in a wok, or frying pan, add the frogs legs, and sauté for 2-3 minutes, until golden in colour. Finely chop the chillies and spring onions and add to the pan together with the sugar and soya sauce. Stir over gentle heat for 2 minutes, then sprinkle in the sesame oil, turn up the heat and cook rapidly for a further 30 seconds.

Sautéed Eel

500 g fresh eel
3 spring onions
1 inch knob fresh ginger
2 cloves garlic
25 ml vegetable oil
1 tablespoon Chinese wine
1 teaspoon light soya sauce
1 teaspoon dark soya sauce
½ teaspoon salt
¼ teaspoon white pepper
2 teaspoons sesame oil

Skin the eel, wash and dry thoroughly, and cut into thin shreds. Finely chop the spring onions and the ginger, and crush the garlic. Heat the oil in a wok, or frying pan, and sauté the ginger and garlic for 2-3 minutes. Add the spring onion, and continue over high heat for a further minute. Then add the eel, Chinese wine, soya sauce, salt and pepper, and cook for a further 5 minutes, stirring continuously. Mix the cornstarch with a little cold water, and add to the pan. Just before serving heat the sesame oil, and sprinkle over the eel.

Turtle with Vegetables

300 g turtle meat
½ teaspoon salt
freshly ground black pepper
25 ml Chinese wine
4 dried Chinese mushrooms
1 green pepper
2 fresh red chillies
2 carrots
1 inch knob fresh ginger
1 clove garlic
50 g bean sprouts
25 ml vegetable oil
25 ml stock
1 tablespoon light soya sauce
1 tablespoon cornstarch
1 teaspoon sesame oil

Chop the turtle meat into small cubes, and boil for 30 minutes. Drain, season with the salt, freshly ground black pepper and Chinese wine, and allow to stand for 30 minutes. Soak the mushrooms in warm water for 30 minutes, remove and discard the hard stems, and chop into small pieces. Finely chop the green pepper, chillies, carrots and ginger, and crush the garlic. Immerse the bean sprouts into boiling water for 1 minute, then remove and drain. Heat the oil in a wok, or frying pan, and sauté the turtle meat for 2-3 minutes, then add all the vegetables, the stock, the reserved marinade and the soya sauce. Continue to cook for a further 3 minutes, stirring continuously. Mix the cornstarch with a small quantity of cold water, and add to the pan. Finally place into a serving dish, heat the sesame oil, and sprinkle over the meat.

Steamed Fish with Ham and Bamboo Shoots

1 fresh white fish, about 600 g
½ teaspoon salt
freshly ground black pepper
1 tablespoon dark soya sauce
1 tablespoon Chinese wine
100 g cooked ham, thinly sliced
200 g canned bamboo shoots

Sauce:
1 brown onion
2 spring onions
25 ml peanut oil
300 ml fish stock
1 tablespoon light soya sauce
¼ teaspoon white pepper
1 teaspoon sugar
dash monosodium glutamate
1 tablespoon cornstarch
1 teaspoon sesame oil

Prepare the fish, and season with the salt, freshly ground black pepper, soya sauce and Chinese wine. Place on a rack, and steam in a tightly sealed container for approximately 6 minutes. Remove the skin and all the bones from the fish, and cut into small slices. Cut the ham into similar size slices. Simmer the bamboo shoots in their own water for 2 minutes, then drain thoroughly and slice. Arrange alternate pieces of fish, ham and bamboo shoot on a serving plate, re-place in the steamer, and cook for a further 2-3 minutes.

To make the sauce, chop the brown onion and spring onions into very small pieces. Heat the oil in a wok, or deep pan, and sauté the onions for 2-3 minutes, until they start to become crispy and turn golden. Then pour in the fish stock, add the soya sauce, white pepper, sugar and mono-sodium glutamate, and simmer gently for 3-4 minutes. Mix the cornstarch with a small quantity of cold water, add to the sauce, and stir for a further minute.

To serve, pour the hot sauce over the fish, ham and bamboo shoots, and sprinkle over the sesame oil.

Fish Fillets in Chilli and Black Bean Sauce

300 g soft white fish fillets
3 tablespoons cornstarch
freshly ground black pepper
½ teaspoon salt
300 ml vegetable oil
50 g fat pork
1 green pepper
2 fresh red chillies
1 spring onion
1 clove garlic
25 g black bean paste
25 ml Chinese wine
50 ml fish stock
1 teaspoon light soya sauce
½ teaspoon dark soya sauce
dash monosodium glutamate

Make certain all the bones have been removed from the fish, and cut into 2 inch pieces. Season with the freshly ground black pepper and salt, and coat with half the cornstarch. Heat the oil in a wok, or large frying pan, until almost smoking, and fry the fish pieces for 2 minutes. Remove from the pan, drain thoroughly, and set aside in a warm place. Pour off most of the oil from the pan. Chop the fat pork, green pepper, chillies and spring onion into small pieces, and crush the garlic. Add these to the pan, together with the black bean paste, and sauté for 2 minutes. Then add the fish pieces, Chinese wine, fish stock, soya sauce and monosodium glutamate, and continue to cook over medium heat for a further minute, stirring well. Mix the remaining cornstarch with a little cold water, and add to the pan. Stir for 1 minute to thicken.

Steamed Fish with Spring Onions

1 fresh fish, about 600 g
½ teaspoon white pepper
1 teaspoon salt
4 spring onions
½ knob fresh ginger
2 teaspoons light soya sauce
2 tablespoons peanut oil

Clean and scale the fish. Make an incision along the underside and remove the backbone to form a pocket, but do not remove the head or tail. Season with the white peper and salt, and allow to stand for 15 minutes. Finely chop 2 of the spring onions and the ginger, and mix with the soya sauce. Stuff the mixture into the prepared pocket of the fish, pour over very hot peanut oil, and place onto a steamer rack. Set the rack over boiling water and steam for 10 minutes. Finally chop the remaining spring onions, scatter over the fish, and continue steaming until cooked.

Sliced Fish in Wine Sauce

1 fish (bream, sole, bass), about
   600 g
freshly ground black pepper
salt to taste
1 egg
2 tablespoons cornstarch
6 dried Chinese mushrooms *
400 ml vegetable oil
100 ml fish stock
25 ml Chinese wine
1 teaspoon light soya sauce
1 teaspoon dark soya sauce
1 teaspoon sugar
2 teaspoons sesame oil

Clean and scale the fish, remove all bones, and cut into slices. Season with the freshly ground black pepper and salt to taste. Beat the egg, mix with 1 tablespoon of the cornstarch, and pour over the fish slices. Place in a refrigerator for 30 minutes. Soak the Chinese mushrooms in warm water for 30 minutes, remove and discard the hard stems, and cut into quarters. Heat the oil in a wok, or deep pan, and fry the fish until half cooked, approximately 2 minutes. Remove the fish, and drain thoroughly. Pour away most of the oil from the pan, and add the Chinese wine, soya sauce and sugar. Replace the fish slices, and cook over low heat for a further 2 minutes. Mix the remaining cornstarch with the fish stock, pour into the pan, and continue to simmer until the sauce thickens slightly and becomes translucent. Pour into a serving dish, and sprinkle over hot sesame oil.

* Note: The original recipe called for the use of a dried Chinese fungus, however as this may not be readily available, the Chinese mushrooms have been substituted in the above recipe.

'Sliced Fish in Wine Sauce' prepared for photography by **American Restaurant,** Wanchai.

Deep Fried Whole Fish with Sweet and Sour Sauce

1 pomfret (or similar fish), about
   600 g
½ teaspoon salt
freshly ground black pepper
1 egg
2 tablespoons cornstarch
500 ml vegetable oil
1 green pepper
2 fresh red chillies
1 inch knob fresh ginger
2 cloves garlic
150 ml fish stock
25 ml Chinese wine
2 tablespoons vinegar
1 tablespoon light soya sauce
1 tablespoon tomato sauce
50 g sugar
75 g canned pineapple pieces

Scale the fish, but do not remove the head or tail. Clean under cold running water, and dry thoroughly. With a sharp knife, score the skin in about 6 places, and season with salt, freshly ground black pepper and monosodium glutamate. Beat the egg and pour over the fish, then coat with half the quantity of cornstarch. Heat the vegetable oil in a wok, or large pan, until almost smoking, and deep fry the fish for 6-8 minutes, until it is cooked, and the skin is crispy and golden brown in colour. Remove the fish, drain off all excess oil, arrange on a serving plate, and keep warm. Chop the green pepper, chillies and ginger, and crush the garlic. Pour away most of the oil from the pan, and sauté the pepper, chilli, ginger and garlic for 2 minutes. Then add the stock, Chinese wine, vinegar, soya sauce, tomato sauce, sugar and pineapple pieces, bring to the boil, and simmer gently for a further 2 minutes. Mix the cornstarch with a little cold water, and add to the pan. Stir until the sauce reaches a desired consistency, then pour over the fish, and serve immediately.

'Deep Fried Whole Fish with Sweet and Sour Sauce' prepared for photography by **Rainbow Room,** Lee Gardens Hotel.

Poultry

雞 鴨

Chicken, duck, pigeon and goose are to be found on the menus of most Hong Kong restaurants, no matter which regional cuisine is being served. However the method of cooking varies a great deal. In Cantonese cooking the birds are most likely chopped, sliced or minced, then braised or stir-fried, and covered with a variety of sauces. While in the North, the birds are more often cooked whole, roasted or baked; the most famous example of this being the delicious Peking Duck. In Szechuan province, no self-respecting chicken would ever be cooked without hot chillies, ginger and garlic.

Barbequed Chicken Livers with Honey

250 g chicken livers
2 teaspoons sugar
25 ml Chinese wine
1 teaspoon dark soya sauce
½ teaspoon salt
¼ teaspoon white pepper
dash monosodium glutamate
50 g honey

Wash the chicken livers, dry thoroughly, and cut into halves. Dissolve the sugar in a small quantity of warm water, then add the Chinese wine, soya sauce, salt, pepper and mono-sodium glutamate. Add the chicken livers to the mixture, stir to coat evenly, and allow to stand for 15 minutes. Place the livers on a skewer, and cook over an open fire for 15 minutes. Remove from the skewer, and place into a shallow dish. Slightly heat the honey, so that it runs smoothly, and pour over the chicken livers.

Chicken Livers baked in Salt

200 g chicken livers
2 spring onions
½ inch knob fresh ginger
25 ml Chinese wine
1 tablespoon dark soya sauce
1 teaspoon sugar
½ teaspoon salt
¼ teaspoon white pepper
1 kilo rock salt

Wash the chicken livers, and dry thoroughly. Chop the spring onions and the ginger into small pieces, and combine with the Chinese wine, soya sauce, sugar, salt and white pepper. Sprinkle the mixture evenly over the chicken livers, and allow to stand for 20 minutes. Heat the rock salt, until it is very hot, then spread a ½ inch layer in the bottom of a wok, or frying pan, place the marinated chicken livers on top, and cover completely with the remaining hot salt. Place a tightly fitting lid on the pan, and bake for 15 minutes.

Chicken baked in Salt

1 chicken, about 1 kilo
2 spring onions
1 inch knob fresh ginger
1 clove garlic
1 tablespoon light soya sauce
1 teaspoon dark soya sauce
25 ml Chinese wine
½ teaspoon salt
¼ teaspoon white pepper
dash monosodium glutamate
2 kilos rock salt

Clean and prepare the chicken. Finely chop the spring onions, ginger and garlic, mix with the soya sauce and Chinese wine, and season with the salt, white pepper and monosodium glutamate. Rub the mixture all over the outside of the chicken, and stuff the remainder inside. Let the chicken stand for 30 minutes, then wrap completely in greaseproof paper. Heat the rock salt in a wok until it is very hot, and place half in the bottom of a large casserole dish. Place the wrapped chicken on top, and pour over the remaining hot rock salt, so that the chicken is completely covered. Place a tight fitting lid on the casserole, and leave for 5-6 minutes. Remove the chicken, re-heat the salt, once again until it is very hot, and repeat the cooking process. Do this a further three times, so that the chicken will have had a total cooking time of between 25 and 30 minutes. To serve, remove the greaseproof paper, and chop the chicken into small pieces.

Chinjew Chicken

500 g fresh chicken meat
½ teaspoon Chinese five-spice
powder
½ teaspoon salt
¼ teaspoon white pepper
1 tablespoon dark soya sauce
50 ml vegetable oil
small bunch parsley *
100 ml chicken stock
1 tablespoon cornstarch
1 teaspoon sesame oil

Chop the chicken meat into small pieces, season with the Chinese five-spice powder, salt, white pepper and dark soya sauce, and let stand for 30 minutes. Heat the oil in a wok, or deep pan, until almost smoking, and deep fry the parsley for 1 minute, until crispy. Remove and drain the parsley, arrange around the edge of a serving platter, and set aside in a warming oven. Re-heat the oil, add the seasoned chicken pieces, and stir-fry for 2-3 minutes. Pour off most of of the oil from the pan, add the stock, and allow to simmer gently for a further 5 minutes. Mix the cornstarch with a quantity of cold water, and add to the pan. Continue to stir for a further 30 seconds, then pour onto serving platter. Finally heat the sesame oil and sprinkle over the chicken.
* Note: The original recipe calls for the use of chrysanthemum leaves, but as it is considered these would not be easily obtained in many cases, parsley has been substituted.

Paper wrapped Chicken

1 chicken, about 1 kilo
2 spring onions
1 inch knob fresh ginger
2 cloves garlic
25 ml Chinese wine
2 tablespoons light soya sauce
1 tablespoon oyster sauce
1 teaspoon sesame oil
1 teaspoon sugar
½ teaspoon salt
¼ teaspoon white pepper
dash monosodium glutamate
500 ml peanut oil

Clean and prepare the chicken, retaining the liver and gizzard. De-bone the chicken, and cut the meat into serving size pieces. Chop the liver and gizzard into small pieces, chop the spring onions and the ginger, and crush the garlic. In a large bowl mix together the chopped liver, gizzard, spring onions, ginger and garlic, and add the Chinese wine, soya sauce, oyster sauce, sesame oil, sugar, salt, pepper and monosodium glutamate. Add the chicken pieces, stir well, and place in a refrigerator to marinate for at least 1 hour. Cut out squares of greaseproof parchment paper, and place a piece of chicken inside each. Wrap up like an envelope, folding in the end flap to secure completely. Heat the oil in a wok, or large pan, until almost smoking, and deep fry the wrapped chicken for approximately 10 minutes, stirring constantly with a slotted spoon. To serve drain off all excess oil, but do not remove paper. Each piece should remain wrapped until the last moment before eating.

Beggar's Chicken

1 fresh chicken, about 1.2 kilos
½ teaspoon salt
6 dried Chinese mushrooms
200 g fat pork
100 g pickled cabbage
1 large brown onion
½ inch knob fresh ginger
1 tablespoon light soya sauce
25 ml Chinese wine
1 teaspoon sesame oil
1 teaspoon sugar
dash monosodium glutamate
freshly ground black pepper
lotus leaves *
400 g pastry dough *

Clean and prepare the chicken, and rub inside and out with the salt. Soak the mushrooms in warm water for 30 minutes, then drain, discard the hard stems, and shred finely. Dice the pork, and chop the pickled cabbage, the onion and the ginger. Fry the fat pork in a wok, or frying pan, until the dices start to become crispy, then add the mushroom, cabbage, onion and ginger. Season with soya sauce, Chinese wine, sesame oil, sugar, monosodium glutamate and freshly ground black pepper, and cook over medium heat for 3-4 minutes, stirring continuously. Remove from the pan, drain off any excess oil, and stuff the mixture inside the chicken. Wrap the stuffed chicken in lotus leaves, and completely seal with the pastry dough. Bake in a very hot oven (475°F: Mark 9) for 1½ hours, then reduce heat and continue cooking for a further 30 minutes. To serve, break away the pastry, and remove the lotus leaves.

*Note: Traditionally the chicken is enclosed in clay rather than pastry, but the latter is simpler, and more usually acceptable for the domestic kitchen. Also if lotus leaves are not readily available, they may be omitted when using pastry, although this would certainly result in some loss of the original flavour.

Supreme Chicken in Lemon Sauce

1 chicken, about 800 g
2 egg yolks
1 tablespoon light soya sauce
3 tablespoons cornstarch
500 ml peanut oil
lemon wedges for garnish

Sauce:
25 ml fresh lemon juice
1 teaspoon sugar
25 ml chicken stock
½ tablespoon cornstarch

With a sharp knife remove all the bones and place the chicken in a shallow dish. Beat the egg yolks, mix with the soya sauce and 1 tablespoon of the cornstarch, and pour over the chicken. Allow to marinate for 10-15 minutes, then remove chicken from the marinade, and coat with the remaining cornstarch. Heat the oil in a wok, or large frying pan, until almost smoking, then deep fry the chicken until golden in colour. Remove and drain thoroughly, then cut into small pieces. Arrange the chicken pieces on a serving dish, pour over the hot sauce, and garnish with the lemon slices.

To make the sauce, mix the lemon juice, sugar and chicken stock, and bring to the boil. Lower heat and simmer until the sugar has completely dissolved. Mix the cornstarch with a little cold water, add to the sauce, and simmer for a further minute to thicken. Pour over the chicken immediately.

'Supreme Chicken in Lemon Sauce' prepared for photography by **Man Wah Restaurant**, Mandarin Hotel.

Chicken with Chillies and Black Beans

500 g chicken meat
1 egg
1 tablespoon cornstarch
½ teaspoon salt
¼ teaspoon white pepper
dash monosodium glutamate
3 fresh red chillies
1 green pepper
2 spring onions
2 small red onions
1 tablespoon preserved black beans
500 ml vegetable oil
100 ml chicken stock
1 tablespoon Chinese wine
1 tablespoon light soya sauce
1 teaspoon sesame oil

Cut the chicken into bite size pieces, and place in a shallow dish. Beat the egg, add the cornstarch, salt, white pepper and monosodium glutamate, and pour over the chicken. Allow to stand for 20 minutes. Chop the chillies, green pepper, spring onions and red onions, and crush the garlic and preserved beans. Heat the oil in a wok, or deep pan, and fry the pieces of chicken for 1 minute. Remove and drain thoroughly. Pour off most of the oil from the pan, add the red onion, garlic and preserved beans, and stir-fry for 1 minute, then add the chillies, green pepper and spring onions, and continue to stir over medium heat for a further 2 minutes. Put back the chicken pieces, and pour in the stock, Chinese wine and soya sauce. Bring to the boil, then simmer gently, until the stock has reduced by half. Arrange in a serving dish, heat the sesame oil, and sprinkle over the chicken.

'Chicken with Chillies and Black Beans' prepared for photography by **Blue Heaven Restaurant**, Central.

Chicken with Dried Red Chillies

400 g chicken meat
8 dried red chillies
2 spring onions
1 inch knob fresh ginger
2 cloves garlic
10 black peppercorns
100 ml peanut oil
½ teaspoon anise powder
25 ml Chinese wine
1 teaspoon light soya sauce
1 teaspoon vinegar
2 teaspoons sugar
½ teaspoon salt
dash monosodium glutamate
½ tablespoon cornstarch
1 teaspoon sesame oil

Cut the chicken meat into small pieces. Soak the chillies in warm water for 30 minutes, cut into halves and remove most of the seeds. Chop the spring onions, ginger and garlic, and crush the peppercorns. Heat the peanut oil in a pan, or deep frying pan, and fry the chicken pieces for 2-3 minutes, then remove, set aside to drain, and pour away three quarters of the oil from the pan. Add the chillies, onions, ginger, garlic, peppercorns and anise powder, and stir-fry until the chillies become crisp and slightly blackened. Add the Chinese wine, soya sauce, vinegar, sugar, salt and monosodium glutamate, and stir for a further minute. Put the chicken pieces back into the pan, and add the cornstarch, mixed with a little cold water. Continue to cook over medium heat for a further 3-4 minutes. After placing in a serving dish, heat the sesame oil, and sprinkle over the chicken.

Chilli Chicken with Cashew Nuts

180 g cooked chicken meat
2 spring onions
1 egg
½ tablespoon cornstarch
40 ml vegetable oil
150 g cashew nuts, shelled
½ teaspoon sugar
½ teaspoon salt
¼ teaspoon white pepper
1 teaspoon cornstarch
1 teaspoon dark soya sauce
1 tablespoon chicken stock
2 cloves garlic
½ inch knob fresh ginger
½ teaspoon chilli powder

Cut the chicken into small dice, and finely chop the spring onions. Beat the egg in a bowl, add the diced chicken, onion and cornstarch, and allow to marinate for 15 minutes. Heat half the oil in a wok, or frying pan, and stir-fry the cashew nuts for 2 minutes, until golden. Remove and set aside. Mix together the sugar, salt, pepper, cornstarch, soya sauce and chicken stock, and add to the pan together with the chicken and marinade liquid. Cook over medium heat for 2-3 minutes, stirring continuously. Remove and set aside. Finely chop the ginger and crush the garlic. In a fresh pan heat the remaining oil, and the ginger, garlic and chilli powder, and sauté for 2 minutes. Finally add the chicken and cashew nuts, and stir for a further 30 seconds to mix together thoroughly.

Diced Chicken with Cashew Nuts

300 g chicken meat
1 egg white
500 ml peanut oil
200 g cashew nuts, shelled
1 tablespoon light soya sauce
1 teaspoon sugar
¼ teaspoon white pepper
salt to taste
200 ml chicken stock
1 tablespoon cornstarch

Cut the chicken meat into small pieces, and coat well with the beaten egg white. Heat the oil in a wok or deep frying pan, and deep-fry the chicken for 2-3 minutes. Remove the chicken pieces, drain well and set aside. Deep fry the cashew nuts for 2 minutes, then pour off most of the oil from the pan, and add the soya sauce, sugar, white pepper and salt to taste. Replace the chicken in the pan, add the stock, and stir over high heat for 2 minutes. Mix the cornstarch with a little cold water, add to the pan and continue to stir for a further minute before serving.

Onion Duck

1 duck, about 1.5 kilos
3 large brown onions
2 spring onions
25 ml light soya sauce
50 ml vegetable oil
250 ml chicken stock
25 ml Chinese wine
2 teaspoons brown sugar
½ teaspoon salt
¼ teaspoon white pepper
1 tablespoon cornstarch

Prepare and wash the duck, and dry thoroughly. Slice the brown onions, and chop the spring onions. Mix the onions with the soya sauce, and stuff inside the cavity of the duck. Secure with thread. Heat the oil in a wok, or large pan, and fry the duck over gentle heat for 10-15 minutes, turning occasionally, to ensure the skin is golden all over. Remove the duck, and drain off all excess oil, then place into a large saucepan, and cover with the stock and an equal quantity of cold water. Bring to the boil, add the Chinese wine, sugar, salt and white pepper, place a lid on the pan, and simmer gently for $1\frac{1}{4}$ hours. Remove the duck, drain thoroughly, and place on a serving dish. Turn up the heat, and rapidly reduce the liquid by half, then mix the corn-starch with a little cold water, and add to the pan. Stir for 1 minute to allow the sauce to thicken slightly, then pour over the duck.

Simmered Duck on Lettuce

1 duck, about 1.5 kilos
2 spring onions
½ inch knob fresh ginger
1 clove garlic
1 tablespoon light soya sauce
1 tablespoon dark soya sauce
25 ml Chinese wine
1 teaspoon brown sugar
¼ teaspoon white pepper
250 ml chicken stock
1 lettuce
25 ml peanut oil
1 tablespoon cornstarch

Prepare and wash the duck, and dry thoroughly. Finely chop the spring onions and crush the ginger and garlic. Mix the onion, ginger and garlic in a bowl with the soya sauce, Chinese wine, sugar and pepper, and rub the mixture all over the surface of the duck. Place any remaining mixture inside the cavity of the duck. Place the duck in a saucepan, and cover with the stock and an equal quantity of cold water. Bring to the boil, then place a lid on the pan, lower the heat, and simmer gently for approximately $1\frac{3}{4}$ hours. Meanwhile, shred the lettuce, fry lighly in the oil and arrange on a serving plate. When the duck is cooked, remove from the pan, drain off excess liquid, break into serving size pieces, and arrange on top of the lettuce. Bring the stock back to the boil, and rapidly reduce by half, then mix the cornstarch with a little cold water, and add to the pan. Stir for 1 minute to allow the sauce to thicken slightly, then pour over the duck.

Sautéed Duck with Ginger

800 g fresh duck meat
½ teaspoon Chinese five-spice
   powder
½ teaspoon salt
¼ teaspoon white pepper
¼ teaspoon baking soda
dash monosodium glutamate
1 inch knob fresh ginger
2 spring onions
25 ml peanut oil
25 ml chicken stock
1 tablespoon Chinese wine
1 tablespoon light soya sauce
1 teaspoon cornstarch

Remove all the skin from the duck, and cut the meat into shreds. Season with the Chinese five-spice powder, salt, white pepper, baking soda and monosodium glutamate, and allow to stand for $1\frac{1}{2}$ hours. Cut the ginger into very thin slices, and cut the spring onions into 1 inch lengths. Heat the oil in a wok, or frying pan, add the shredded duck meat, and sauté for 2 minutes. Add the ginger, and continue to stir for a further minute. Then pour off most of the oil, add the stock, Chinese wine and soya sauce, and simmer for 4-5 minutes, stirring occasionally. Finally mix the cornstarch with a small quantity of cold water, and add to the pan to thicken sauce slightly.

Breasts of Duck with Mushrooms

2 breasts of duck
¼ teaspoon baking soda
2 teaspoons dark soya sauce
4 dried Chinese mushrooms
1 clove garlic
500 ml vegetable oil
50 ml chicken stock
1 tablespoon Chinese wine
2 teaspoons light soya sauce
¼ teaspoon white pepper
1 tablespoon cornstarch
1 tablespoon chopped spring onion

Remove the skin from the duck breasts, and cut diagonally, through the bone, into thin slices. Sprinkle the baking soda and the dark soya sauce over the duck, and let stand for 1 hour. Soak the mushrooms in warm water for 30 minutes, remove and discard the hard stems, and cut into shreds. Crush the clove of garlic. Heat the oil in a wok, or large pan, until it is almost smoking, then deep fry the duck pieces for 2-3 minutes. Remove the duck, and allow to drain. Pour off most of the oil from the pan, add the garlic, and sauté for 30 seconds. Then put back the pieces of duck, pour in the stock, Chinese wine and soya sauce, and add the white pepper. Allow to simmer for 5-6 minutes, over low heat. Mix the cornstarch with a small quantity of cold water, add to the pan, and cook for a further minute, stirring in thoroughly. Arrange in a serving dish, and sprinkle the chopped spring onions over the duck.

Steamed Stuffed Duck

1 duck, about 1.5 kilos
1 teaspoon salt
freshly ground black pepper
250 g fresh pork
25 g lard
4 dried Chinese mushrooms
4 spring onions
1 brown onion
1 inch knob fresh ginger
2 cloves garlic
2 teaspoons light soya sauce
1 teaspoon dark soya sauce
¼ teaspoon Chinese five-spice
  powder
500 ml vegetable oil

Clean and prepare the duck, and after washing, dry thoroughly. Season with the salt and freshly ground black pepper. Chop the pork into small dice, and fry gently in the lard for 2-3 minutes. Remove the pork, and allow to drain. Soak the mushrooms in warm water for 30 minutes, remove and discard the hard stems, and cut into thin slices. Chop the spring onions, brown onion and ginger, and crush the garlic. Mix these together with the diced pork, and season with the soya sauce and Chinese five-spice powder. Stuff the mixture inside the duck, and secure with a needle and cotton. Heat the vegetable oil in a wok, or large pan, until it is almost smoking, and deep fry the duck for 3-4 minutes, until the skin is golden brown and crispy. Remove, drain off all excess oil, place in a tightly sealed container, and steam for 4 hours.

Peking Duck

1 fat duck, about 1.5 kilos
120 g golden syrup
1 tablespoon honey
1 tablespoon light soya sauce

Pancakes:
200 g plain flour
½ teaspoon salt
200 ml boiling water
1 tablespoon sesame oil
4 spring onions
½ cucumber
50 g Hoi Sin (sweet plum) sauce

Clean and prepare the duck, leaving on the head. Wash inside and out, dip into a pan of rapidly boiling water for a few seconds, then dry thoroughly. Mix the syrup, honey and soya sauce with a little water, and bring to the boil. Coat the duck inside and out with the syrup mixture. Place a string around the duck's neck and hang in a draughty place for 4-5 hours. (If preferred, an electric fan may be used to stretch the skin more quickly.) Place the duck in a pre-heated oven (375°F: Mark 5) for approximately $1\frac{1}{2}$ hours, turning occasionally to make sure the skin is dark brown and crispy all over. To serve, wrap pieces of the skin in a pancake together with a piece of spring onion, a thin stick of cucumber and some Hoi Sin sauce.

To make the pancakes, sift the flour and salt into a mixing bowl, and make a well in the centre. Slowly pour in the boiling water, and gradually mix into the flour to form a soft dough. Knead gently for 10 minutes until the dough becomes pliable, then cover with a damp cloth, and allow to stand for 10 minutes. Roll out to $\frac{1}{4}$ inch thickness, and cut into 2 inch circles. Brush one side with sesame oil, and place 2 pancakes together with the oiled sides facing each other. Roll out into larger circles. Heat a large heavy frying pan, or a skillet, and cook pancakes for 2 minutes, turning once. Peel pancakes apart and stack on a warmed plate.

'Peking Duck' prepared for photography by **Princess Garden Restaurant**, Kowloon.

Minced Pigeon wrapped in Lettuce

2 pigeons
40 g cooked chicken liver
4 dried Chinese mushrooms
60 g bamboo shoots
2 spring onions
½ inch knob fresh ginger
2 eggs
1 tablespoon cornstarch
1 tablespoon light soya sauce
1 teaspoon sugar
dash monosodium glutamate
½ teaspoon white pepper
salt to taste
50 ml peanut oil
25 ml Chinese wine
1 teaspoon oyster sauce
1 lettuce
Hoi Sin (sweet plum) sauce

Prepare the pigeons, and boil until tender. Take care to remove all the bones, then mince the meat. Soak the mushrooms in warm water for 30 minutes and discard the hard stems. Chop the mushrooms, bamboo shoots, spring onions and ginger into very small pieces. Dice the chicken liver. In a large bowl beat the eggs, and add the cornstarch, soya sauce, sugar, monosodium glutamate, pepper and salt to taste. Place the pigeon meat and the chicken liver into the bowl, and allow to stand for 15 minutes. Heat the oil in a wok, or frying pan, and stir-fry the meat for 2-3 minutes. Remove and drain. Add the mushrooms, bamboo shoots, spring onions and ginger to the pan, and sauté for 2 minutes, then replace the meat, add the Chinese wine, oyster sauce and marinade, and stir over medium heat for a further 3 minutes. Rectify seasoning to taste, and, if necessary, thicken with a little extra cornstarch mixed with cold water. Place onto a large serving plate. Separate the lettuce leaves, and eat by spooning a little meat onto each lettuce leaf and adding a small quantity of 'Hoi Sin' (sweet plum) sauce.

'Minced Pigeon Wrapped in Lettuce' prepared for photography by **Rainbow Room**, Lee Gardens Hotel.

Baked Stuffed Pigeon

2 pigeons, about 500 g each
1 teaspoon salt
freshly ground black pepper
dash monosodium glutamate
4 dried Chinese mushrooms
1 large brown onion
3 spring onions
1 clove garlic
75 g fresh shrimps
25 ml vegetable oil
1 egg
2 teaspoons dark soya sauce
1 teaspoon oyster sauce
25 ml Chinese wine
1 tablespoon cornstarch
50 g butter

To prepare the pigeons, cut along the backbone and remove the carcass, leaving the leg and wing bones intact. Spread the pigeons open, and season with the salt, freshly ground black pepper and monosodium glutamate. Soak the mushrooms in warm water for 30 minutes, and discard the hard stems. Chop the mushrooms, brown onion, spring onions and crush the garlic. Shell and de-vein the shrimps, and pass through a fine mincer. Heat the oil in a wok, or large frying pan, and stir-fry the vegetables and shrimps for 2-3 minutes. Remove from the pan, and drain off all excess oil. Beat the egg, add the soya sauce, oyster sauce, Chinese wine and cornstarch, and mix thoroughly with the vegetables and shrimps. Spread the mixture evenly over the insides of the pigeons, then close up to re-shape the birds, and secure with bands of greaseproof parchment paper. Pour off most of the oil from the pan, add the butter, and bring almost to the boil. Add the pigeons, lower heat slightly, and cook for 5-6 minutes, turning frequently to ensure the skin is crispy and golden brown all over. Then place a lid on the pan, and continue over medium heat until the pigeons are cooked. During this latter stage it may be necessary to add a little extra oil to avoid sticking.

* Note: If preferred, the final stage of cooking may be done in a steamer.

Sliced Pigeon with Mushrooms and Bamboo Shoots

300 g cooked pigeon meat
freshly ground black pepper
½ teaspoon salt
½ teaspoon sugar
dash meat tenderizer
2 dried Chinese mushrooms
100 g bamboo shoots
100 ml vegetable oil
25 ml Chinese wine
25 ml chicken stock
1 teaspoon oyster sauce
1 teaspoon light soya sauce
dash monosodium glutamate
1 tablespoon cornstarch
1 teaspoon sesame oil

Cut the pigeon meat into thin slices, and season with the freshly ground black pepper, salt, sugar and tenderizer. Let stand for 30 minutes. Soak the mushrooms in warm water for 30 minutes, discard the hard stems and cut into thin slices. Cover the bamboo shoots with cold water, bring to the boil, and cook for 3-4 minutes. Drain and cut into small pieces. Heat the oil in a wok, or frying pan, and fry the piegon meat for 5 minutes, stirring occasionally. Remove the pigeon, allow to drain, and pour off most of the oil from the pan. Toss the mushroom and bamboo shoots in the small quantity of remaining oil for 30 seconds, then replace the slices of pigeon, and add the Chinese wine, chicken stock, oyster sauce, soya sauce and monosodium glutamate, and continue to cook for a further 2 minutes. Mix the cornstarch with a little cold water, and add to the pan, stirring until the sauce thickens. Finally sprinkle on the sesame oil just before serving.

Meats
肉 類

Pork and beef are by far the most
common meats used in Chinese
cooking. Veal is hardly ever used, and
recipes calling for lamb generally
originate from the far Northern
frontier regions. Game is eaten on
special occasions, but seldom seen at
other times. Most meat dishes involve
chopped, sliced or shredded meat,
often marinated in spices and Chinese
wine, and cooked with a variety of
vegetables. Only seldom are large
pieces of meat grilled or roasted.

Pork Liver with Vegetables

300 g pork liver
1 egg
2 teaspoons cornstarch
1 teaspoon light soya sauce
1 teaspoon peanut oil
3 dried Chinese mushrooms
50 g bean sprouts
2 leeks
2 spring onions
1 clove garlic
50 ml vegetable oil
25 ml chicken stock
1 tablespoon tomato sauce
½ teaspoon salt
freshly ground black pepper

Wash the liver, and cut into thin slices. Beat the egg, mix with half the cornstarch, light soya sauce and peanut oil, and pour over the pork. Soak the mushrooms in warm water for 30 minutes, and discard the hard stems. Immerse the bean sprouts in boiling water for 1 minute, then remove and drain. Cut the leeks diagonally into $\frac{1}{2}$ inch pieces, chop the spring onions and the mushrooms, and crush the garlic.
Heat the oil in a wok, or frying pan, add the liver, and stir-fry over very high heat, for 2 minutes. Lower the heat, add the stock, tomato sauce and all the vegetables, and season with the salt and freshly ground black pepper. Simmer for 2-3 minutes, then mix the remaining cornstarch with a small quantity of cold water, and add to the pan. Stir for a further minute.

Special Spiced Pork

300 g lean fresh pork
½ teaspoon salt
¼ teaspoon white pepper
¼ teaspoon Chinese five-spice
   powder
dash monosodium glutamate
1 egg
50 g breadcrumbs
50 ml vegetable oil
1 large brown onion
1 green pepper
2 tomatoes
2 fresh red chillies
1 inch knob fresh ginger
1 clove garlic
50 ml chicken stock
1 tablespoon Chinese wine
1 tablespoon tomato sauce
2 teaspoons cornstarch
1 teaspoon sesame oil
1 tablespoon chopped spring onion

Cut the pork into thin slices, about 2 inches long, and season with the salt, white pepper, Chinese five-spice powder and monosodium glutamate. Beat the egg, pour over the pork, then roll the pieces of pork in the breadcrumbs. Heat the oil in a wok, or frying pan, until it is very hot, and stir-fry the pork for 2-3 minutes, until golden brown. Remove, drain off excess oil, and keep warm. Slice the brown onion, add to the pan, and sauté for 1 minute, then chop all the remaining vegetables, add to the pan, and stir-fry for a further 2 minutes. Pour in the stock, Chinese wine and tomato sauce, put back the pieces of pork, and simmer for 2-3 minutes. Mix the cornstarch with a small quantity of cold water, and add to the pan. Finally add the sesame oil, and chopped spring onions, and stir to mix in thoroughly.

Sweet and Sour Pork

250 g lean pork
1 teaspoon salt
freshly ground black pepper
1 teaspoon sugar
¼ teaspoon Chinese five-spice
   powder
1 egg
2 tablespoons cornstarch
500 ml vegetable oil

Sauce:
1 brown onion
1 green pepper
2 carrots
1 tomato
1 inch knob fresh ginger
2 cloves garlic
1 fresh red chilli
50 g canned pineapple chunks
200 ml chicken stock
25 ml vinegar
1 tablespoon light soya sauce
1 tablespoon tomato sauce
1 tablespoon lemon juice
2 teaspoons sugar
dash monosodium glutamate
1 tablespoon cornstarch

Cut the pork into serving pieces, and season with the salt, freshly ground black pepper, sugar and five-spice powder. Beat the egg, pour over the pork, and allow to marinate for 30 minutes. Remove the pork, and coat all pieces evenly with the cornstarch. Heat the oil in a wok, or large heavy pan, and deep fry the pork pieces, until they are cooked, and golden brown in colour, approximately 5 minutes. Remove, drain thoroughly, and keep warm.

To make the sauce, roughly chop the onion and pepper, slice the carrots and tomato, crush the ginger and garlic and cut the chilli into thin shreds. Pour off most of the oil from the pan the pork was fried in, and sauté the onion until golden, Add the pepper, carrot, tomato, ginger, garlic and chilli, and stir-fry over high heat for 1 minute. Then pour in the stock, and add the pineapple chunks, vinegar, soya sauce, tomato sauce, lemon juice, sugar and monosodium glutamate. Bring to the boil, and simmer for a further 3 minutes. Mix the cornstarch with a small quantity of cold water, and add to the sauce to thicken. Finally add the pork pieces to the sauce, and allow to heat through thoroughly.

Spareribs with Black Beans and Chillies

300 g pork spareribs
freshly ground black pepper
salt to taste
1 clove garlic
4 fresh red chillies
4 fresh green chillies
1 green pepper
1 inch knob fresh ginger
1 carrot
30 g fermented black beans
25 ml vegetable oil
2 tablespoons dark soya sauce

Cut the spareribs into $1\frac{1}{2}$ inch pieces, and season with freshly ground black pepper and salt to taste. Crush the garlic, chop the chillies, pepper and ginger and slice the carrots. Heat the oil in a wok, or large pan, add the garlic and black beans and sauté for 3 minutes. Lower the heat and add 50 ml. of warm water. Place in the spareribs, cover the pan, and simmer for 3-4 minutes. Remove the cover, add the chillies, pepper, ginger and carrot, increase the heat and continue to cook for a further 2 minutes, stirring well. Place in a serving dish and sprinkle with the soya sauce.

'Spare Ribs with Black Beans and Chillies' prepared for photography by **Lychee Village Restaurant**, Kowloon.

Pork and Pickled Cabbage with Sesame Buns

250 g lean fresh pork
½ teaspoon salt
¼ teaspoon white pepper
4 dried Chinese mushrooms
100 g canned pickled cabbage
100 g green peas
25 ml peanut oil
1 tablespoon Chinese wine
2 teaspoons light soya sauce
1 teaspoon dark soya sauce
1 teaspoon sugar
1 teaspoon sesame oil

Sesame buns:
150 g plain flour
25 ml peanut oil
¼ teaspoon dry yeast
25 g sugar
1 tablespoon dark soya sauce
1 teaspoon light soya sauce
1 teaspoon sesame seeds

Chop the pork into very small pieces, and season with the salt and white pepper. Soak the mushrooms in warm water for 30 minutes, then drain and discard the hard stems. Soak the pickled cabbage in cold water for 30 minutes, drain, cover with fresh water, and bring to the boil for 3 minutes. Drain thoroughly, then chop the cabbage and mushrooms. Cover the peas with cold water, bring to the boil for 3 minutes, and drain. Heat the oil in a wok, or frying pan, add the pork, and stir-fry for 2-3 minutes. Then add the mushrooms, cabbage and peas, and season with the Chinese wine, soya sauce and sugar. Stir over medium heat for a further 3 minutes. Heat the sesame oil, and sprinkle over the mixture, then place on a serving platter, and keep warm while preparing the sesame buns.

To prepare the buns, first heat the oil in a small pan, and mix in one quarter of the flour. Blend thoroughly and set aside. Dissolve the yeast in approximately 50 ml. of warm water, add nearly all the remaining flour, and mix to form a pliable dough. Cover with a clean cloth, and allow to rise for 30 minutes, before rolling out to approximately $\frac{1}{4}$ inch thickness. Spread the originally blended flour and oil on top, and sprinkle over the small remaining quantity of flour. Shape into a roll, about 2 inches in diameter, cut into $1\frac{1}{2}$ inch slices, and place onto a lightly greased baking tray. Dissolve the sugar in a small quantity of warm water, mix in the soya sauce, and brush the buns with the mixture. Finally sprinkle over the sesame seeds, and bake in a moderate oven for 10-15 minutes, until light golden in colour. To serve, cut a pocket in each bun, and fill with a quantity of the pork and cabbage mixture.

'Pork and Pickled Gabbage with Sesame Buns' prepared for photography by **Peking Garden Restaurant**, Causeway Bay.

Roasted Pork

800 g fillet of pork
2 small red onions
1 inch knob fresh ginger
100 ml chicken stock
50 ml Chinese wine
1 tablespoon light soya sauce
1 tablespoon dark soya sauce
1 teaspoon sugar
¼ teaspoon white pepper
1 tablespoon honey

Pork Chops with Abalone

4 pork loin chops
50 ml chicken stock
50 ml Chinese wine
1 tablespoon dark soya sauce
50 ml Chinese wine
1 tablespoon dark soya sauce
1 tablespoon light soya sauce
½ inch knob fresh ginger
½ teaspoon salt
freshly ground black pepper
50 g chopped chives
25 ml vegetable oil

Cut the pork into pieces, approximately 2 inches wide, 2 inches thick and 6 inches long. Chop the onions into small pieces, and cut the ginger into thin slices. Add the onion and ginger to the stock, together with half the Chinese wine, soya sauce, sugar and white pepper. Blend thoroughly, pour over the pork, and place in a refrigerator to marinate for at least 12 hours. Remove the pieces of pork, drain off any excess liquid, and place on a metal rack set in a roasting pan. Reserve the marinade. Place the pork into a pre-heated moderately hot oven (400°F: Gas Mark 6), and roast for 20-25 minutes. Stir the honey into the reserved marinade and add the remaining Chinese wine. Place the partly cooked pork back into the marinade, and set aside for 30 minutes. Finally replace the pork in the oven, and cook for a further 10-15 minutes.

Trim off excess fat from the chops, and season with the salt and freshly ground black pepper. Cut the abalone into small slices. Pour the stock into a wok, or frying pan, together with half the Chinese wine and the soya sauce. Bring to the boil, add the pork chops, and simmer very slowly until the liquid has almost completely reduced. Remove the chops and place on a metal rack set in a roasting pan. Chop the spring onion, and crush the ginger and garlic, and mix with the remaining Chinese wine. Spread the mixture over the pork chops, and place in a pre-heated oven (425°F: Gas Mark 7) for 10-15 minutes. Meanwhile, pour the oil into the pan in which the pork chops were cooked, add the abalone, and stir-fry over high heat for 6 minutes. Finally add the celery, and continue to stir over reduced heat for a further 2-3 minutes. To serve, place the chops on a serving platter, and spoon over the abalone and celery.

Pork and Bean Sprouts

200 g fresh pork
1 egg
½ tablespoon light soya sauce
1 tablespoon Chinese wine
1 teaspoon sugar
½ teaspoon salt
¼ teaspoon white pepper
dash monosodium glutamate
2 teaspoons cornstarch
2 dried Chinese mushrooms
150 g bean sprouts
3 spring onions
2 cloves garlic
25 ml peanut oil

Discard any excess fat from the pork, and cut into fine shreds. Beat the egg and mix with the Chinese wine, soya sauce, sugar, salt, pepper, monosodium glutamate and cornstarch. Pour the mixture over the pork, and allow to stand for 1 hour. Soak the mushrooms in warm water for 30 minutes; remove, drain and discard the hard stems. Cut the bean sprouts into 1½ inch lengths, chop the mushrooms and spring onions, and crush the garlic. Heat the oil in a wok, or frying pan, until very hot, add the pork, and stir fry for 15-20 seconds. Remove, and drain off most of the oil from the pan. Then put back the pork, together with the mushrooms, bean sprouts, spring onions and garlic. Lower heat, and stir fry for a further 3-4 minutes.

Minced Pork Balls with Cabbage

400 g fresh pork
½ teaspoon salt
¼ teaspoon white pepper
1 teaspoon light soya sauce
dash monosodium glutamate
2 eggs
200 g chopped cabbage
200 ml chicken stock
freshly ground black pepper
1 tablespoon cornstarch

Mince the pork, and season with salt, pepper, soya sauce and monosodium glutamate. Beat the eggs, mix with the pork, and divide into small balls. Heat the oil in a wok, or frying pan, and cook over medium heat until the pork balls are cooked and are golden brown all over. Remove from the pan, and keep warm. Add the cabbage to the pan, and stir-fry for 1-2 minutes. Pour in the stock, bring to the boil, replace the pork balls, season with the freshly ground black pepper, and simmer until the stock has reduced by half. Mix the cornstarch with a little cold water, and add to the pan to thicken the remaining sauce.

Ground Spiced Beef with Bean Curd

200 g ground beef
1 tablespoon Chinese wine
2 teaspoons dark soya sauce
½ teaspoon salt
¼ teaspoon white pepper
100 g bean curd
2 small red onions
3 fresh red chillies
1 inch knob fresh ginger
2 cloves garlic
1 tablespoon fermented black beans
100 ml vegetable oil
50 ml beef stock
1 tablespoon oyster sauce
1 tablespoon chilli sauce
1 tablespoon light soya sauce
1 tablespoon cornstarch
1 teaspoon sesame oil
2 spring onions

Mix the ground beef with the Chinese wine, dark soya sauce, salt and white pepper, and allow to stand for 20 minutes. Cut the bean curd into 1 inch square pieces. Chop the red onions, chillies and ginger, and crush the garlic and black beans. Heat the oil in a wok, or deep pan, and fry the bean curd for 2-3 minutes, stirring frequently. Remove, and drain off excess oil. Pour off most of the oil from the pan, add the beef, onions, chillies, ginger, garlic and black beans, and stir-fry for 2 minutes. Then pour in the stock, and add the chilli sauce and the light soya sauce, and simmer gently for a further 2 minutes. Mix the cornstarch with a small quantity of cold water, and add to the pan, and at the same time put back the pieces of bean curd. Stir well for 1 minute, then sprinkle in the sesame oil, and arrange in a serving dish. Finally, cut the spring onions into 1 inch lengths, and place on top.

Fried Beef with Oysters

200 g lean beef
25 ml Chinese wine
½ teaspoon salt
freshly ground black pepper
dash monosodium glutamate
8 fresh oysters
1 teaspoon fresh lemon juice
1 inch knob fresh ginger
2 cloves garlic
100 ml vegetable oil
1 teaspoon dark soya sauce
1 teaspoon light soya sauce
50 ml beef stock
1 tablespoon cornstarch
1 tablespoon chopped spring onions

Cut the beef into small thin slices, pour over half the Chinese wine, season with the salt, freshly ground black pepper and monosodium glutamate, and let stand for 30 minutes. Open the oysters carefully, and retain the oyster water. Sprinkle the remaining Chinese wine and the fresh lemon juice over the oysters, and let stand for 5 minutes. Chop the ginger and garlic into very small pieces. Heat the oil in a wok, or frying pan, until very hot, and fry the beef for 1 minute. Remove, and drain off excess oil, and pour off most of the oil from the pan. Add the oysters to the pan, stir-fry gently for 2 minutes, then remove and keep warm. Add the ginger and garlic, and sauté for 1 minute, then put back the beef, and pour in the retained oyster water, soya sauce and the stock. Simmer for 2-3 minutes, then mix the cornstarch with a small quantity of cold water, and add to the pan. Return the oysters to the pan, and continue to cook gently for a further minute. After arranging in a serving dish, sprinkle over the chopped spring onions.

Sliced Beef with Green Peppers and Black Bean

200 g lean beef
½ teaspoon salt
freshly ground black pepper
1 teaspoon sugar
¼ teaspoon baking soda
dash monosodium glutamate
1 tablespoon dark soya sauce
1 tablespoon peanut oil
2 large green peppers
2 cloves garlic
½ tablespoon fermented black beans
200 ml vegetable oil
1 tablespoon oyster sauce
1 tablespoon light soya sauce
1 tablespoon Chinese wine
1 tablespoon cornstarch
2 teaspoons sesame oil

Cut the meat into small, thin slices. Season with the salt, freshly ground black pepper, sugar, baking soda, monosodium glutamate, dark soya sauce and peanut oil, and let stand for 1 hour. Remove the seeds from the green pepper, and chop into fairly large pieces, and crush the garlic. Heat the oil in a wok, or large heavy pan, until it is almost smoking, then deep fry the beef for approximately 20 seconds. Remove and drain the beef, and pour off most of the oil from the pan. Put the meat back in the pan, together with the green pepper, garlic and fermented black beans, and stir-fry over medium heat for 1-2 minutes. Add the oyster sauce, light soya sauce and Chinese wine, and continue to stir for a further minute. Mix the cornstarch with a small quantity of cold water, and add to the pan. Serve immediately onto a platter, then heat the sesame oil, and sprinkle over the beef.

Sliced Beef with Mushrooms and Bamboo Shoots

200 g lean beef
½ teaspoon salt
¼ teaspoon white pepper
dash monosodium glutamate
6 dried Chinese mushrooms
50 g canned bamboo shoots
2 spring onions
1 clove garlic
25 ml peanut oil
1 tablespoon light soya sauce
1 tablespoon Chinese wine
1 tablespoon cornstarch

Cut the meat into small thin slices, and season with the salt, pepper and monosodium glutamate. Soak the mushrooms in warm water for 30 minutes, remove and discard the hard stems, and cut into slices. Drain the liquid from the canned bamboo shoots, and slice thinly. Chop the spring onions, and crush the garlic. Heat the oil in a wok, or frying pan, and sauté the meat gently for 1-2 minutes, until it is well browned. Add the mushrooms, bamboo shoots, spring onions and garlic, and stir-fry over high heat for 20 seconds. Lower the heat, add the soya sauce, Chinese wine and 25 ml. of water, and allow to simmer for a further 5 minutes. Mix the cornstarch with a small quantity of cold water, add to the pan, and stir in thoroughly.

Chinese Style Fillet Steak

250 g fillet steak
2 brown onions
2 spring onions
1 inch knob fresh ginger
2 cloves garlic
dash monosodium glutamate
½ teaspoon salt
¼ teaspoon white pepper
1 teaspoon sugar
1 tablespoon light soya sauce
50 ml Chinese wine
1 tablespoon custard powder
2 egg whites
25 ml vegetable oil
1 tablespoon tomato paste

Cut the meat into 2 inch pieces and remove all excess fat. Slice the brown onions, chop the spring onions and ginger and crush the garlic. Place the meat and vegetables into a dish, and add the monosodium glutamate, salt, pepper, sugar, soya sauce and Chinese wine. Mix the custard powder with a small quantity of cold water to make a smooth paste, then slowly beat in the egg whites and blend thoroughly. Pour evenly over the meat and vegetables, and allow to stand for 30 minutes.

Heat the oil in a wok, or large pan, pour in the meat, vegetables and marinade, and cook over medium heat for 3-4 minutes, stirring continuously. Remove the pieces of meat and arrange on a serving plate, then add the tomato paste to the ingredients in the pan, stir well for a further minute and pour over the meat.

Sliced Beef with Crispy Batter

150 g lean beef
1 teaspoon cornstarch
1 teaspoon light soya sauce
¼ teaspoon white pepper
50 g crispy fried batter
2 spring onions
½ inch knob fresh ginger
40 ml peanut oil
1 egg
½ teaspoon sugar
1 tablespoon Chinese wine
1 teaspoon dark soya sauce
¼ teaspoon salt
25 ml beef stock

Cut the beef into small thin slices, sprinkle over the cornstarch, light soya sauce and white pepper, and let stand for 20 minutes. Cut the crispy fried batter into small cubes. Chop the spring onions, and crush the ginger. Heat the oil in a wok, or frying pan, and sauté the beef for 1 minute. Add the ginger and spring onions, and continue to stir over medium heat for 2 minutes. Beat the egg, and mix with the remaining cornstarch, sugar, Chinese wine, dark soya sauce, salt and beef stock. Add the mixture to the pan together with the pieces of crispy fried dough, blend thoroughly, and simmer for a further 2 minutes.

Shredded Beef in Taro Nest

250 g fillet steak
½ teaspoon white pepper
½ teaspoon salt
25 ml Chinese wine
200 g taro *
1 egg, beaten
2 tablespoons cornstarch
500 ml vegetable oil
1 green pepper
1 brown onion
50 g bamboo shoots
½ inch knob fresh ginger
2 fresh red chillies
2 cloves garlic
1 teaspoon sugar
1 tablespoon light soya sauce
2 teaspoons oyster sauce

Cut the beef into fine shreds, season with pepper and salt, pour over the Chinese wine, and allow to stand for 15 minutes. Cut the taro into fine shreds, and coat with a mixture of the beaten egg and half the cornstarch. Arrange the shredded taro in a frying basket in the shape of a nest, and deep fry in very hot oil for 3-4 minutes, until golden. Set aside and keep warm. Pour off most of the oil. Chop the green pepper, onion, bamboo shoots, ginger and chillies, and crush the garlic. Add the vegetables to the pan with the remaining oil, and sauté for 2-3 minutes. Add the beef, remaining marinade, sugar, soya sauce and oyster sauce, and continue to cook over medium heat for a further 5-6 minutes, stirring constantly. Mix the cornstarch with a little cold water, add to the pan and blend in thoroughly. Pour into the taro nest, and serve immediately.

*Note: Potato may be substituted for the taro, if the latter is not available.

'Shredded Beef in Taro Nest' prepared for photography by **Tsui Hang Village Restaurant**, Miramar Hotel.

Vegetables

菜類

Many main dishes, fish, poultry and meat, include vegetables, but even so, a well balanced Chinese meal should always include a vegetable dish in its own right. This will very often be a mixed dish, with the cross blending of many different vegetables, and the use of spices resulting in a rich and appetising flavour. Very little water is used, and the cooking time is minimal. Never, never, would a good Chinese cook boil away the natural goodness. Some vegetables found in the markets of Hong Kong may not be available elsewhere, certainly not outside Asia, and for that reason some substitutions have been made. Naturally, however, the use of local and seasonal vegetables, should always take priority when planning the menu.

Vegetable display photographed at **Jade Garden Restaurant**, Star House, Kowloon.

Braised Assorted Vegetables with Brown Sauce

6 dried Chinese mushrooms
2 carrots
3 water chestnuts
8 button mushrooms
4 fresh white mushrooms
6 baby corn cobs
small bunch leaf spinach
1 inch knob fresh ginger
50 g crispy fried batter
50 ml peanut oil
25 ml Chinese wine
1 teaspoon salt
½ teaspoon white pepper
1 teaspoon sugar
dash monosodium glutamate
1 tablespoon light soya sauce
2 teaspoons dark soya sauce
1 tablespoon cornstarch
1 teaspoon sesame oil

Soak the mushrooms in warm water for 30 minutes, drain and discard the hard stems, and cut into quarters. Wash and drain all the other vegetables, cut the carrots and water chestnuts and ginger into thin slices, and dice the crispy batter. Heat the oil in a wok, or frying pan, add the vegetables¹, pieces of batter and Chinese wine, and stir over medium heat for 2 minutes. Pour in 100 ml. of cold water, and season with the salt, pepper, sugar, monosodium glutamate and soya sauce. Bring back to the boil, then simmer for a further 5 minutes. Mix the cornstarch with a small quantity of cold water, and add to the pan, to thicken the sauce. After pouring into a serving dish, heat the sesame oil, and sprinkle over the vegetables.

Cabbage with Cream Sauce

1 large Chinese cabbage *
½ teaspoon salt
25 ml vegetable oil
50 ml fish or chicken stock
1 tablespoon cornstarch
25 ml milk
1 slice cooked ham
1 tomato

Remove the outer leaves from the cabbage, and place into a pan of cold water. Add the salt, bring to the boil, and allow to simmer for 20 minutes. Remove and rinse under cold running water for 1 minute, then cut into strips, and arrange on a serving dish. Heat the oil in a pan, and slowly pour in the stock. Mix the cornstarch with the cold milk until smooth then add to the pan, and cook for 1 minute, stirring continuously. Pour over the cabbage. Shred the ham, cut the tomato into small dice, and sprinkle on top.
* Note: If the long Chinese cabbage is not available, the regular round cabbage is an acceptable substitute.

Eggplant in Hot Garlic Sauce

1 eggplant (aubergine), about 500 g
2 spring onions
1 inch knob fresh ginger
2 fresh red chillies
3 cloves garlic
100 ml peanut oil
60 g shredded beef
1 tablespoon light soya sauce
1 teaspoon sugar
½ teaspoon salt
¼ teaspoon white pepper
100 ml stock
2 teaspoons cornstarch
1 teaspoon vinegar
1 teaspoon sesame oil

Wash the eggplant, and cut, on the bias, into thin slices. Chop the spring onions, ginger and chillies, and crush the garlic. Heat the oil in a wok, or frying pan, and gently fry the eggplant for 3-4 minutes, until soft. Remove from the pan, and drain off all excess oil. Pour away most of the remaining oil from the pan, and add the onions, ginger, chillies, garlic and shredded beef. Stir well for 1 minute, then add soya sauce, sugar, salt, pepper and stock. Bring to the boil, add the eggplant, lower heat, and simmer until the liquid has been reduced by half. Mix the cornstarch with a small quantity of cold water, and add to the pan to thicken the sauce. Finally just prior to serving, stir in the vinegar and the sesame oil.

Broccoli and Lettuce in Wine and Oyster Sauce

250 g broccoli spears
1 lettuce
200 ml vegetable oil
500 ml chicken stock
25 ml peanut oil
25 ml Chinese wine
25 ml oyster sauce
1 tablespoon light soya sauce
1 tablespoon dark soya sauce
2 tablespoons cornstarch
50 g shredded cooked ham

Wash the vegetables under running water. Dry the broccoli thoroughly. Heat the vegetable oil in a wok, or large pan, and fry the broccoli spears for 2 minutes. Remove and drain off excess oil. In a large saucepan, bring the stock to the boil, add the broccoli, and simmer for 3 minutes. Remove and drain, and place the whole lettuce in the stock. Again, simmer for 3 minutes. Remove, drain, tear off the leaves, and place with the broccoli in a serving dish. Set aside in a warming oven. In a fresh pan, heat the peanut oil, add the stock, Chinese wine, oyster sauce and soya sauce, and bring to the boil. Mix the cornstarch with a small quantity of cold water, and add to the pan. Simmer gently for 1-2 minutes, until the sauce has thickened, then pour over the broccoli and lettuce. Finally sprinkle the shredded ham over the vegetables.

Sweet Flavours
甜品

With Chinese meals, simple or formal, at home or in the restaurant, elaborate dessert dishes do not play the important part they do in the West. This is particularly true of the Cantonese cuisine, where the meal is usually completed with fresh fruit, or with a simple fruit-based dish requiring little preparation. Not surprisingly most of the hot and filling sweet dishes have originated in the Northern and Western regions, where the weather is considerably colder than in the South.

Bird's Nest with Melon Balls

150 g dried bird's nest
50 g sugar
½ watermelon *

Soak the bird's nest in cold water for a period of at least 5 hours. Remove any impurities, rinse thoroughly and allow to drain. Using a small scoop make a quantity of balls from the watermelon, and set aside in a refrigerator. In a large saucepan pour in 600 ml. of water and bring to the boil. Add the sugar, and stir until completely dissolved. Remove from the heat, and allow to chill before adding melon balls.
*Note: Honeydew melon or grapes may be substituted.

Bird's Nest in Coconut

150 g dried bird's nest
40 g sugar
50 ml coconut milk

Soak the bird's nest in cold water for a period of at least 5 hours. Remove any impurities, rinse thoroughly and allow to drain. Bring 500 ml. of water to the boil, add the bird's nest, sugar and coconut milk, and allow to boil rapidly for 3-4 minutes. Serve immediately.

Yam and Pumpkin Dessert

200 g yam (or sweet potato)
200 g pumpkin
1 tablespoon lemon juice
100 g sugar
1 teaspoon cinnamon powder
25 ml vegetable oil
1 spring onion, chopped
1 teaspoon chopped orange zest

Peel the yam and pumpkin, and cut into ½ inch cubes. Place in a saucepan and add just sufficient water to cover. Bring to the boil and allow to simmer for 20 minutes. Remove from the pan, drain thoroughly, sprinkle over the lemon juice, add the sugar and let stand for 3-4 hours. Then place in a tightly sealed container, and steam for 40 minutes. Drain off the juice into a fresh pan, add cinnamon powder, and simmer until liquid reduced by half. Heat the oil in a wok, or frying pan, and fry the onion for 1 minute. Remove and discard onion (purpose is to give oil flavour), then add the yam, pumpkin, juice and orange zest. Stir over medium heat until all the oil has been absorbed.

Candied Yam

200 g yam (or sweet potato)
100 g sugar
2 teaspoons lemon juice
1 teaspoon grated orange peel
500 ml peanut oil
1 teaspoon sesame seeds

Cut the yam into ½ inch cubes, and place in a saucepan. Sprinkle over the sugar, add the lemon juice and approximately 50 ml. of water, and bring to the boil. Add the grated orange peel, lower heat, and stir until the sugar has caramelised. Remove, cut into pieces, and allow to set. Heat the peanut oil in a large pan until almost smoking, then add the pieces of candied yam, and deep fry for 2 minutes. Remove, drain off any excess oil, and sprinkle over the sesame seeds.

Szechuan Date Pancakes

150 g dates
150 g sugar
100 g sweet bean paste
25 ml peanut oil

Pancakes:
150 g plain flour
25 ml milk
2 eggs
25 g butter
½ teaspoon sugar
500 ml vegetable oil

Chop the dates into small pieces, and place in a saucepan together with the sugar. Add just sufficient water to cover, bring to the boil, and simmer gently for 4-5 minutes, until the sugar has all dissolved. Pass through a fine sieve, and mix with the sweet bean paste. Heat the peanut oil in a wok, or frying pan, add the mixture, and stir for 2-3 minutes over low heat. Remove and drain away all excess oil.

Make a thin batter by mixing together the flour, milk, eggs and butter. If the batter is too thick add a little extra milk or cold water. Add a little batter to a large greased frying pan, or skillet, and cook until just set. Remove, and repeat until all the batter has been used. Spread equal portions of the date mixture into the centre of each pancake, fold and seal. Heat the vegetable oil in a wok, or deep pan, and deep fry the pancakes until golden in colour. Cut into 3 inch pieces to serve.

Toffee Apples and Bananas

2 large cooking apples
3 bananas
100 g plain flour
500 ml vegetable oil
100 ml peanut oil
150 g sugar
25 g sesame seeds
iced water

Peel and core the apples, and cut into wedges. Skin the bananas and cut into quarters, first lengthways, then across. Mix the flour with sufficient water to form a smooth batter, and coat the apple and banana pieces. Heat the vegetable oil in a wok, or large pan, and deep fry the fruit for 2-3 minutes, until golden in colour. In a saucepan, heat the peanut oil, add the sugar and 100 ml. of water, and stir until the sugar is all dissolved. Add the fried apple and banana pieces, and mix until they are evenly coated with the syrup. Remove, sprinkle with the sesame seeds, and plunge immediately into the iced water to set the syrup hard.

'Toffee Apples and Bananas' prepared for photography by **American Restaurant**, Wanchai.

Almond Jelly with Fruits

25 g agar agar (gelatine)
100 g sugar
1 teaspoon almond powder
150 ml sweetened evaporated milk
300 g canned fruit salad

Place the agar agar and half the sugar into a large saucepan, and pour over 500 ml. of cold water. Slowly bring to the boil, and allow to simmer for 10 minutes. Add the almond powder, and continue to simmer for a further 10 minutes. Add the remaining sugar, and pour in the evaporated milk, and stir until the sugar has completely dissolved. Pour the mixture into a lightly greased shallow cake tin, allow to cool, then place in the refrigerator, and leave to set firmly. Before serving, cut the almond jelly into diamond shapes, or squares, place in a serving bowl together with the fruit salad, and stir gently to combine. Serve chilled.

'Almond Jelly with Fruits' prepared for photography by **Man Wah Restaurant**, Mandarin Hotel.

Acknowledgements

In producing this revised edition, sincere appreciation is once again due to the
HONG KONG TOURIST ASSOCIATION, and to Hong Kong's own 'discovery' airline,
CATHAY PACIFIC, for their continuing enthusiastic assistance and support.

Many thanks also to all the friendly 'gourmets', too numerous to permit individual mention,
whose advice and guidance (based on years of great gastronomic experience!), helped me
decide which recipes to include. I regret that through lack of space, some will find their
favourite flavours missing, but this has been unavoidable.

Finally, it must be acknowledged that, without the help of many of Hong Kong's leading
restaurateurs and chefs, nothing would have been possible. Listed below are the restaurants
from which a large percentage of the recipes contained within this edition originated. Where
photographs were taken, additional acknowledgements appear on the appropriate pages.

American Restaurant, 23 Lockhart Road, Wanchai.	5-277277
Blue Heaven Restaurant, 38 Queen's Road, Central.	5-243001
Fung Lum Restaurant, 20 Leighton Road, Causeway Bay.	5-777669
Gay Tops Restaurant, International Hotel, Cameron Road, Kowloon.	3-663381
Golden Lotus Restaurant, Hilton Hotel, Queen's Road, Central.	5-233111
Great Shanghai Restaurant, 6A Prat Avenue, Kowloon.	3-668158
Jade Garden Restaurant, Star House, Kowloon.	3-661326
Lao Cheng Hsing Restaurant, 9 Stanley Street, Central.	5-244722
Lo Fung Restaurant, Peak Tower, The Peak.	5-96688
Luk Kwok Restaurant, 67 Gloucester Road, Wanchai.	5-270721
Luk Yu Teahouse, 24 Stanley Street, Central.	5-235464
Lychee Village Restaurant, 9 Cameron Road, Kowloon.	3-686444

Restaurant	Phone
Man Wah Restaurant, Mandarin Hotel, Connaught Road, Central.	5-220111
Mayflower Restaurant, 6 Tonnochy Road, Wanchai.	5-724311
Miramar Theatre Restaurant, Miramar Hotel, Nathan Road, Kowloon.	3-681111
Oceania Restaurant, Ocean Terminal, Kowloon.	3-670181
Pak Lok Restaurant, 23 Hysan Avenue, Causeway Bay.	5-768886
Peking Garden Restaurant, Excelsior Shopping Arcade, Causeway Bay.	5-777231
Peking Restaurant, 144 Gloucester Road, Wanchai.	5-754212
Pleasure Restaurant, 45 Carnarvon Road, Kowloon.	3-660408
Rainbow Room, Lee Gardens Hotel, Hysan Avenue, Causeway Bay.	5-767211
Red Pepper Restaurant, 7 Lan Fong Road, Causeway Bay.	5-768046
Riverside Restaurant, Food Street, Causeway Bay.	5-778010
Sea Palace Floating Restaurant, Aberdeen.	5-525112
Siam Birds Nest Restaurant, 55 Paterson Street, Causeway Bay.	5-770967
Sky King Restaurant, 655 Nathan Road, Kowloon.	3-961566
Siu Lam Kung Restaurant, 22 Hanoi Road, Kowloon.	3-669238
Sze Chuen Lau Restaurant, 466 Lockhart Road, Causeway Bay.	5-792571
Tien Heung Lau Restaurant, 18C Austin Avenue, Kowloon.	3-662414
Tsui Hang Village Restaurant, Miramar Hotel, Nathan Road, Kowloon.	3-681111
Wishful Cottage Restaurant, 336 Lockhart Road, Causeway Bay.	5-735645
Yaik Sang Restaurant, 456 Lockhart Road, Causeway Bay.	5-766211
Yung Kee Restaurant, 32 Wellington Street, Central.	5-232343

Index